Healing from the consequences of

Accident, Shock
and Trauma

ELLEL MINISTRIES
THE TRUTH & FREEDOM SERIES

Healing from the consequences of
Accident, Shock and Trauma

Peter Horrobin

Founder and International Director of Ellel Ministries

Sovereign World

Sovereign World Ltd
Ellel Grange
Bay Horse
Lancaster
Lancashire LA2 0HN
United Kingdom

www.sovereignworld.com
Twitter: @sovereignworld
Facebook: www.facebook.com/sovereignworld

First published April 2016, this edition 2019

ISBN: 978-1-85240-743-8

Cover design & typesetting by Zaccmedia.com
Printed in the Great Britain by Bell and Bain Ltd, Glasgow

Contents

Preface   6
Foreword   9

Part 1

Accident, Shock and Trauma: Understanding the Problem   11

1   Jim and Lynda's Stories   13
2   Our Journey of Understanding   19
3   What Can Happen When We Have
    an Accident   35
4   So What Actually *is* Trauma?   45
5   Stories from the Coalface   53
6   The 'Bus Accident'   65
7   How and Why Inner Brokenness
    Occurs   77
8   Broken-heartedness   87

Part 2

Accident, Shock and Trauma: Applying God's Solution   101

9   Building on a Good Foundation   103
10 Forgiveness: The Doorway of Hope   117
11 The Key of Deliverance   131
12 Healing the Broken-hearted   139
13 Healing for Victims of Wartime Traumas   147
14 Epilogue   155

Further Resources   159

Preface

This is a book which provides real answers to a real problem – God's answers from the teaching of Scripture for those who have suffered the consequences of accident, shock and trauma. And these answers have been well-proven through thirty years of exciting experience, praying with people on every continent of the world.

In 1970, as I was surveying the wreck of a pre-war Alvis sports car, I sensed the Lord was speaking to me. As I looked at the vandalized remains of the vehicle, I was overwhelmed with a sense that the world was full of hurting people – many of whom, like this car, were desperately in need of restoration, having been devastated by the traumatic experiences of life. I prayed into this vision for sixteen years until a work of healing was established at Ellel Grange in 1986, which became known as Ellel Ministries.

When the work started, we were first taken on a journey of understanding, discovering what is broadly termed the inner healing ministry. Then we wrestled with understanding deliverance and why, as in the ministry of Jesus, deliverance was sometimes a necessary part of healing. It was a very challenging but at times very exciting journey, as step-by-step we discovered keys to healing from the Scriptures that were truly life-transforming.

One of the most profound of these Scriptural keys unlocked the problem of why many people were still suffering the unseen consequences of accidents, shocks and traumas many years after the event. In Isaiah 61:1 we read that the Sovereign Lord (Jesus) would *"heal the broken-hearted"* (GNB) and when the Lord showed us how to minister this truth into people's lives, we suddenly began to see major healing breakthroughs. People who had not only suffered physically, but had been broken on the inside by the trauma they had experienced, began to make dramatic recoveries from even long-term conditions.

The accidents and traumas that people have experienced are many and varied, ranging through car accidents, falling off horses or down stairs, fires, birth complications, sudden loss of a close family member, military action, emotional shocks, sports injuries, natural disasters and even being attacked by wild animals! The list of things that have happened to people, which have left an indelible, unhealed scar on their lives, is almost beyond description.

But whatever the original cause of their problem, there is one common denominator in the lives of all these people; they have been traumatized and broken on the inside. And it is in those precious words from Isaiah 61:1 that the key to their healing lies.

I pray that this book will be a blessing to those who have their own particular needs resulting from accidents, shocks and traumas in their lives. But I pray, also, that it will provide those who have the privilege of ministering the healing love of Jesus to people, with vital keys to making their work even more effective.

I am deeply grateful to every single member of the Ellel Ministries teams with whom it has been my privilege to work across the years. They have all contributed to the contents of this book by faithfully ministering the truths of Scripture into the lives of those who have come through the doors of Ellel Ministries centers looking to God for help.

I am especially grateful to Lynda Scott for writing the Foreword. Lynda is one of those whose life was massively transformed through the application of the teaching this book contains. She is no longer suffering from the consequences of a catastrophic fall from a cliff, which had given her a lifelong expectancy of being disabled and had earned her a lifetime disability pension. After many disappointments it took a huge step of faith for her to risk asking for prayer just one more time. And God healed her – she is no longer disabled and no longer needs or has the pension! Thank you, Lynda, for the enormous contribution to our understanding of how God heals the broken-hearted that came through praying for you.

I am especially thankful to God for my wife, Fiona, with whom I have shared the journey of faith that this book represents. Time and time again her insights, understanding and discernment have been used by the Lord to achieve real breakthroughs in the lives of countless people. This book could not have been written without her.

The constant support and input from Ellel Ministries team members, many of whom read and reread the manuscript, offering important suggestions for improving the script, was a critical part of the writing process – huge thanks to everyone who helped.

But above all, I am deeply thankful to the Lord for opening our eyes to see the wonderful truths in His Word, and for His work of healing which has transformed the lives of so many people. I give Him heartfelt praise and thanks for everything He has done.

Peter Horrobin
Ellel Grange, Lancaster, LA2 0HN, England
February 2016

Foreword

Lynda Scott

Author of *Lynda: From Accident and Trauma to Healing and Wholeness*

I first heard the teaching contained in this book twenty years ago. I had suffered a major accident three years previously and was having to live with the dreadful consequences. But as I listened to the teaching, my heart came to life! Because what I heard meant that for a person like me, for whom the doctors had said *"there's nothing more that we can do for you,"* there was hope. Real hope of healing! And after I received prayer I was completely healed by Jesus!

You will find as you read this book many stories of real people's lives, including my own. Stories of people who, when the principles from God's Word were applied with love, faith and prayer, received healing from Jesus. Let these stories build your faith and as you identify with the people whose lives they describe, let them prepare your own heart to receive Jesus' healing too.

I believe that Peter's biblical teaching, understanding and application to bringing healing to victims of accident and trauma is revolutionary. It is good news and needs to be shared with everybody! There are so many broken and hurting people in our world who suffer in silence and believe there is nothing more that can be done for them. Maybe you are one. This book is a beacon in the darkness. Jesus loves each one of us so deeply and He truly does have the answers for every broken heart.

I know you will be blessed as you read this book, and I expect you will be blessed in ways you are not even expecting! Come with an open heart now and let the Holy Spirit speak to you through its pages.

Lynda Scott
January 2016

Accident, Shock and Trauma:Understanding the Problem

This book has been divided into two parts. This first part seeks to explain what happens when people suffer traumatic experiences caused by accidents, shocks or, on occasions, very abusive situations. Understanding what is happening on the inside provides important life-transforming keys for praying with people.

It was the understanding that is shared in the first half of the book that made it possible for us to pray for Lynda, who wrote the Foreword to the book, and many others.

In the second part of the book, I will provide a series of key steps for you to take when praying for healing for others or when applying the teaching to your own life.

Jim and Lynda's Stories

"I can breathe! I can breathe!"

I will never forget Jim's excited cry as he looked up at me, in total amazement, saying, "I can breathe! I can breathe!" Jim had been a chronic asthmatic since the age of six and now God was healing his asthma. He was able to breathe normally and freely for the first time that he could remember!

Jim and his wife had been listening to the teaching on accident and trauma, but at first they were not thinking about Jim's asthma, they were asking another question. Could it be that there was an answer for the symptoms Jim had wrestled with for much of his life? For seventeen years he hadn't been able to lift his right arm above his shoulder.

Jim was thirty-four when he had been sitting on his tractor in the farmyard. A large piece of timber fell from the roof of the barn and hit him on the shoulder, pushing him off the tractor. As he fell to the ground, his knee pushed the tractor into gear and the tractor began to move forward. The large rear wheel of the machine climbed over Jim's back, just missed his head and rolled over his right shoulder, before pursuing its driverless journey across the yard.

Jim's badly damaged shoulder was put back together by the doctors, but it never fully healed and he remained unable to lift that arm above shoulder height. Because he could easily have been killed in the accident and was so grateful for not having lost his life, he regarded the loss of movement in his arm as a relatively minor inconvenience!

But God didn't consider the damaged shoulder to be a minor inconvenience and by the end of the evening Jim was waving his arm in the air, having experienced a miracle of healing. What the doctors had been unable to do following the accident, God had done, seventeen years later!

But that wasn't all God healed that night as a result of prayer about trauma. By the end of the evening the asthma, which had been such a restrictive curse on Jim's life, was totally gone as well! He went for a brisk walk in the cold night air of a Canadian winter and suffered no asthmatic symptoms. And when I met Jim's wife many years later, she was able to say that his symptoms never came back. God did two miracles for Jim that night. In a later chapter I will tell more of how God healed him so profoundly on that never-to-be-forgotten occasion.

No Longer Disabled

Lynda had been a nurse in Australia, but following a catastrophic accident had been unable to work for 18 months, then only very limited duties for the following year. She had fallen 35 feet off a cliff and fractured her back in four places. When Fiona and I first met her, Lynda was on heavy medication for the constant pain from her back and was unable to walk properly. She was also suffering from chronic fatigue and was losing hope.

She was registered as disabled by the Australian government and had been placed on a lifetime disability pension. She had been given no expectation by the medics that she would ever be able to walk properly again and live a normal life and had been suicidal, having convinced herself that there was no further point in living. She saw no prospect of ever being off painkillers and all hope of marriage, children and grand-children had disappeared out of the window in her rapidly disintegrating life.

We met Lynda at a Christian medical conference organized by Health Care in Christ. We tried to encourage her to believe that God could heal her. But when asked if she would like us to pray for her healing, she politely declined, saying she didn't want any more prayer – because she didn't want to find out again that God didn't love her. The prospect of not being healed yet again was more than she could bear. Her response was totally understandable, but we had seen God heal the consequences of accidents and traumas on many occasions, and we encouraged her to trust God once more for her healing.

When ministering back in the UK, the Lord had shown us the principles of praying for people who were unhealed following accidents or traumas. I explained to Lynda that in Isaiah 61:1 the prophet had said that the Sovereign Lord would heal the broken-hearted and this means much more than just being deeply upset or grieving. When we have an accident, it isn't just the body that gets broken, our heart can also be traumatized and we can be broken on the inside as well. We explained how the medics are only able to do everything they can to heal the broken body, but healing the broken heart was outside the range of medical practice. For the heart, only Jesus is the healer.

We patiently spent time explaining the healing principles to her, and told her stories of people who had been wonderfully healed from even long-term consequences of accidents and traumas. She was especially impacted by Jim's story of the healing of his broken shoulder and the asthma he had suffered since the age of six as a result of prayer for the inner trauma.

I was scheduled to teach on healing from the consequences of accident and trauma at the conference that night and by the time of the meeting, Lynda had very hesitantly and bravely agreed to be prayed for one more time, and in front of an audience of medical professionals.

For two hours, Fiona and I prayed with her about all the issues surrounding the accident, helping her to forgive the person who had led her into a dangerous situation where the accident had happened, and delivering her from the fears and infirmities that had invaded her life as a result. God was bringing healing to the inner depths of Lynda's being.

If our inner being is broken and hurting then our body reflects that inner pain. But when God heals the broken heart, there is no pain to reflect and the body can then be healed as well.

At the end of that time of inner healing and deliverance ministry, I anointed Lynda with oil for healing, according to the Scriptures, and everyone watched as they saw God work a physical miracle before their very eyes. I sensed the Lord was telling us to stand back and watch what He did. No one was touching her as her body was being stretched, as if by angels, who came down and gave her divine 'physiotherapy.' Her back was supernaturally moved backwards and forwards. It was being healed and restored.

At the end of the evening, Lynda's face was absolutely radiant, the pain had gone and she could walk normally. The following morning she was no longer fatigued, but rose early to walk to a prayer room at the top of a hill and give thanks to God for her healing. Previously she had been unable to walk more than a few yards, without having to stop to let the pain subside.

Later, Lynda went back to the government authorities, told them she was healed and today she is no longer disabled, no longer on a lifetime pension, and is married with three wonderful children. A full account of Lynda's amazing story, including a transcript of the prayer ministry that night, is now told in her own book, *Lynda: From Accident and Trauma to Healing and Wholeness,* also published by Sovereign World.

Both Jim and Lynda were terribly traumatized by their accidents, but that did not prevent God from healing them. What God did for them both was truly miraculous. Through the pages of this book I want to share with you the principles of healing from the consequences of accident, shock and trauma. We will return, therefore, to look at both Jim and Lynda's healing in greater depth in later chapters.

You will discover that God is still doing miracles today as he heals the broken-hearted, transforms broken lives and sets the captives free. What He has done for others He can do for you too.

Our Journey of Understanding

As a young man I was passionate about old Alvis sports cars. I used post-war models for my day-to-day transport for many years, but the Alvis that I dreamed of owning was a pre-war open touring model known as an Alvis Speed 20. They were rare and expensive and I doubted if I would ever be able to own one, but one day a friend offered me one that needed restoring. He was only asking for £50! That was within my budget, so I acquired the wreck of a car that had been stolen, crashed, vandalized, set on fire and finally pushed into the River Mersey, near Liverpool.

I began work on restoring the car on the 18th of June 1970, but as I looked at the remains of what was formerly a beautiful Alvis Speed 20 sports car, I noticed, to my dismay, that the chassis was bent. There were tears in my eyes as I began to see my dream of a restored Speed 20 melt away. It was at that moment, however, that God spoke to me so very clearly and said, *"You could restore this broken car, but I can restore broken lives."* He then asked me, *"Which is more important, a broken car or a broken life?"*

The answer was obvious and ever since that moment God has had me on a journey of understanding of how to apply the truths of His Word into the lives of those who have been hurt and damaged on the road of life.

As it was, the car was useless and undrivable. With a bent chassis it could never be steered in a straight line or be safely stopped. It had suffered a major accident and, you might say, it was very traumatized! In order to begin the work of restoring the car I needed a blueprint of the chassis design from the maker, so that the chassis could be straightened and the car could be rebuilt according to the master plan. With that in my hand the work could begin.

And the work of restoring broken lives is very similar. There are many people who are struggling to cope with life, and are unable to function as God intended, because of things that have happened to them in the past. In order to begin the work of restoration, we need to have a blueprint of what the Maker (God) intended. If we try to do it our way we will always, ultimately, fail. God has a strategy and a plan (a blueprint) for the journey of faith on the road to healing.

So, before I explain more about trauma and accidents, it's important that I share with you some of the important steps that we had to take along the road on our journey of understanding of God's blueprint for restored lives.

Welcome, Teach and Heal

During those years of praying, before Ellel Ministries began in 1986, the Lord gave me a particular vision for a regular series of Healing Retreats, and how they should be run. We would have five relational teaching sessions to explain essential healing principles, followed by personal prayer and ministry for the people on the retreat. I was looking in the Bible for what we should teach on each session and was reading Luke's Gospel chapter 9. When I had gotten to verse 11, it was as if my reading had suddenly been halted by a red traffic light! STOP – don't go any further, this is it. You've found the treasure – now read it – again and again and again. *"Jesus welcomed the people, he spoke to them about the Kingdom of God and healed those in need of healing.*"

I had never noticed before the logical significance of how the careful Dr. Luke had described what Jesus was doing. Here was the key to finding the blueprint I was looking for. First, Luke said, *"Jesus welcomed the people."* That word 'welcome' embraces a whole heap of meaning. But in essence a welcome is a practical expression of love. If people are loved and welcomed, they are a hundred times more likely to listen to what you have to say.

Jesus didn't just want us to teach words, He first wanted people to know that they were loved. Why else was it that people from every level of society flocked to listen to Jesus and to receive from Him? There was love in His eyes, love in His voice and people were able to receive His, and Father God's, love. Showing love to people had to be the first step in God's strategy, otherwise it would not be a ministry of healing.

I read on. *"Jesus spoke to them about the Kingdom of God."* This was the ultimate key I was looking for in asking the question, "What should we teach on our Healing Retreats?" When I saw it, it was so obvious I was spiritually kicking myself for having previously been so blind! God didn't want us to teach people about healing, but to show them love and tell them about the Kingdom of God, and what it really means to live one's life according to His Kingdom principles.

I remembered how John the Baptist had said *"Repent, for the Kingdom of God is at hand."* A modern version of these important words says, *"Get your life in order for the King is coming!"* And that didn't mean any old king, it meant the King of God's Kingdom, the Son of God, the King of kings!

Over the years we have seen how many of those who come for help are living very disordered lives – lives which are a long way from what God intended for His children. Most have known no better, because no one had taught them the truths that are in God's Word. It's no surprise, therefore, that their lives were still in need of deep-level healing. Sometimes the disorder has been a consequence of the circumstances that people have endured at the hands of others. And in their need, people search for an answer to their problem and sometimes, even, can be tempted to do things which need to be undone before the real work of praying into the traumas of their life can begin.

Finally I came to the last part of Luke 9:11, *"and Jesus healed those in need of healing."* There was a definite sequence here – show love, teach about the Kingdom of God, help them get their lives into God's order, and then pray with them for healing. God's blueprint for the practice of the ministry was slowly emerging and I was really excited. Luke 9:11 was to become the foundational Scripture for the whole of the ministry. It was as if God had spoken to me with an audible voice out of the pages of Scripture. I now knew the direction we would need to be going.

Next, I had to start preparing the Kingdom-based teachings for each session of a Healing Retreat. The first would certainly need to include teaching about making Jesus Lord of our lives – for without that, how can anyone get their lives into godly order? And after that there was the need to be forgiven for all that is past and also to forgive all those who have hurt us.

The teaching was coming together – but I needed to practise. Who shall I practice on? I decided to practice on sheep! I used to exercise the dogs on a flat piece of grassy shore-land. Here there were always lots of sheep and in my mind they represented the very first people who would receive the Kingdom teaching on a Healing Retreat. After all, Jesus had talked about people as if they were sheep, so it didn't seem too far off-track to be teaching sheep as if they were people!

I laughed at myself as I spoke out the teaching into the air. I looked at the faces of the sheep – they were all different – and, extraordinarily, God began to show me, in my mind's eye, the very different faces of dozens of individual people, representing the hundreds of people who would come on future retreats.

Hurts and pains so often lie behind the facial signals people give out. I had to grow in discernment, and understand more about what God sees when He looks into our faces and into our hearts. I realized that if we could learn to see as He sees, then the work would be so much easier!

At the end of John chapter 2 it says that Jesus *"did not need man's testimony about man, for he knew what was in man."* No wonder Jesus's healing ministry was always so effective – He knew exactly what the people's problems were as He looked into their faces and into their hearts. His prayers were spot on every single time!

As a result, I've learned to ask the Lord to show me what lies behind the faces of those who come for prayer. Faces are often very revealing and can tell their own story of how the person has lived or has been treated by others on their journey through life.

First Steps

It was a really exciting but nerve-wracking day when we finally welcomed the first guests into Ellel Grange for our very first Healing Retreat. But God in His graciousness had gone ahead of us and we were incredibly blessed by all that He did. Val, for example, had suffered severe traumas when she was young. As a result she tried to solve the consequences of what had happened by taking control of everything she could – including of her eating habits. As a result, she became a chronic anorexic.

For the previous fourteen years, Val hadn't eaten any solid food – her diet was liquids only. Her condition was so bad that her husband could not tolerate the relationship any longer. He was ready to throw her out and divorce was imminent. She was desperate and suicidal. For Val, there was no point in living any more. Life for her was hell on earth. She had come to the end of herself. One day she went into a local church and did a deal with God – telling Him that unless He did something soon, she was going to take her own life.

On her way out of the church she noticed a leaflet about a new ministry that was opening up at Ellel Grange. She noted the phone number and telephoned for help. She tells me now that I invited her to come on the first Healing Retreat and on hearing that she was suicidal, I said, "Well, why don't you wait until after the retreat to do it!" Not exactly the best counseling advice, but I was in faith that God would so impact her life on the retreat that afterwards she wouldn't want to commit suicide! And that's exactly what happened.

On the first night of the retreat she realized that she needed Jesus to be her Lord and Savior and she invited Him into her life. On the next day she faced the issues which had led to her becoming anorexic, experienced God's healing and was delivered of the demonic powers that were driving her to suicide. Her anorexia was already beginning to be a thing of the past.

On the final day of the three-day retreat, fifteen inches of snow fell and she couldn't get home. She had to call the husband who didn't want her back and ask him to come and get her. She told him she was now very different. Reluctantly he came, but his car had gotten stuck in the thick snow in the Ellel Grange drive and he had to walk into the building and telephone for the Automobile Association to come and tow him out. It took four hours for them to get there.

In those four hours we fed both him and Val. He watched in total shock and amazement as he saw this lady who, for fourteen years, had only ever drunk liquids, consume a full plate of fish and chips! She was so radically changed and healed that he came back on a retreat for himself a few weeks later. He placed his faith and trust in Jesus also and then they went off to Bible college together. For the next twenty years, Val was a Salvation Army evangelist and pastor. Today, in her retirement from pastoral work, she is a highly valued member of the ministry team at Ellel Grange, praying that God will do for others what He did for her on that very first retreat thirty years ago.

Having seen what God did for Jim, Lynda and Val and having witnessed first-hand God healing literally hundreds of people, I began to realize that many of their symptoms had their roots in all kinds of different traumas and accidents, and I can say with great confidence that Jesus heals today. When we choose to put our lives into godly order and agree in faith with the teaching of Scripture, we are preparing the ground for God to move in power in our lives and restore our inner disorder and brokenness.

Those first few weeks, months and years of the ministry proved to be a unique on-the-job training school. As with any learning experience we didn't get everything right first time and sometimes had to backtrack in our thinking – but always God continued to show us His understanding of what we were seeing in people's lives and how to walk with them on their healing journey.

Frequently we came up against people with symptoms that had been prayed for many times, but which were not responding to prayer. People would come on healing retreats with very familiar stories such as, "I've already been prayed for many times, but God hasn't healed me." Their words were often accompanied by heart cries of desperation and looks of sadness on their faces. When we unpacked what they were saying, we realized that in most cases it was their symptoms that had been prayed for many times, not the root cause of the problem.

Praying for Symptoms or Healing the Root?

Ever since the first day of the ministry we had been on a dramatic learning curve as we realized that, for most people, the symptoms they were experiencing weren't actually the underlying problem. The symptoms were what people were suffering, but the reasons why they had the symptoms lay elsewhere.

In my younger days, I spent a lot of time working on old cars. Their bodywork often showed signs of rust coming through. It was easy to clean off the surface rust, spray on some fresh paint, give it a polish and think the job was done. But not many weeks, and sometimes only days later the tell-tale signs of rust would once again be appearing in the very place that had been covered by the freshly sprayed paint! Such 'instant' treatments never lasted. To deal with the problem, it was always necessary to fully expose the underlying surface, remove every trace of rust from the bare metal, treat the metal with rust-inhibiting paint, then properly cover any holes with filler, before finally rubbing down the surface and spraying with several coats of new paint.

Praying for people's symptoms, without exposing and treating the real needs, is a bit like painting over rust. The person might feel good for a short time, but before very long the symptoms usually return and continue to dominate their lives. And, sadly, when that happens they can sometimes lose hope and trust in God – even to the extent, like Lynda, that they give up believing for their healing and don't want to risk having any more prayer like that because, in their experience, it doesn't work.

As we worked with many different individuals, with a huge range of presenting problems, little by little God began to show us the many different root causes that could be behind their symptoms. It was not unusual to find that similar presenting symptoms could have a number of different root causes. For example, we were often asked to pray for couples who had been unable to conceive. This was the presenting symptom – the 'rust,' if you like – but when we scraped away the 'rust' we discovered there were many different possible causes of the problem and each one needed to be prayed for in a different way.

It is the same God who heals, but just as Jesus dealt with people in very different ways, so must we. With some of the people Jesus prayed for, He simply spoke healing into their bodies. Others he touched. Some were delivered of an evil spirit and yet others received both deliverance and healing. We began to understand the need for the gift of discernment, which Paul lists as one of the gifts of the Holy Spirit in 1 Corinthians 12:7–11.

Without the Holy Spirit's help we would be praying healing for different people in exactly the same way, time and time again, but without much success. For some people that prayer may be appropriate, almost by chance, but for the majority we would simply be blessing them with a prayer, but without having any real expectation that they would or could be healed. We were beginning to see that the largest single reason that people are not healed when they are prayed for is because we are praying for the wrong thing and the real issues causing the problem are not being faced or resolved.

I remember praying for a lady with a residual neck problem, following a car accident that had taken place many years previously. It was only when the Lord prompted me to ask why she was in the car at the time of the accident that the real key to her healing was revealed. She then confessed that she had been on her way to commit adultery when the accident occurred. Until this unconfessed sin had been dealt with before the Lord, it wasn't possible for her to receive the healing that God longed to give her.

We need to take careful note of all the relevant Scriptures. In James 5:16, James says: *"Therefore confess your sins to each other and pray for each other so that you may be healed."* Here James was highlighting a real problem that he had clearly experienced, 2,000 years ago. For some people their unconfessed and unforgiven sin was an obstacle to their healing. This is no different today. What Scripture teaches as sin is still sin today and we cannot ignore the need for dealing with it if we are truly wanting God's healing.

The more we prayed with people the more we began to understand the underlying principles of healing. Where God's order had been violated, it was necessary for the person to bring things into line with His order for their life, before they could receive all the blessings He has in store for them. Patterns began to emerge as we saw how one particular set of circumstances in a person's life would regularly lead to a similar set of symptoms. As we began to apply the lessons God was teaching us, there was a dramatic increase in the effectiveness of the praying. For example, where a person had embraced an ungodly belief system or a wrong relationship, when the issue was dealt with through confession, forgiveness and repentance, the prayer for healing was, suddenly, much more effective!

Discovering the Accident Problem

There was one pattern, however, that emerged from hundreds of hours of prayer, with many different people, that left us with more questions than answers! There were a lot of people with long-term physical symptoms, and no obvious reason as to why they were not being healed through prayer. Many of these people had suffered accidents at some time in their past. Thanks to the medical treatment they had received at the time, they had made huge progress on their road to healing, but somehow or other their healing journey had gotten 'stuck,' for want of a better word, and they had learned to live with, and even be content with, the measure of healing they had received and their residual symptoms.

For example, Karel had fallen off a bus when he was a child, injuring his head and his neck. In adult life he accommodated himself to the ongoing pain by walking with a slight stoop, which, in time, became his permanent bodily position; Dorothy had fallen between the platform and a train on the London underground and her arm had been wrenched out of its socket. The medics put it all back together OK, but she had to be content with never being able to lift things with that arm or move the arm around normally. Just like Jim and Lynda, Karel and Dorothy had been prayed for many times for their ongoing symptoms, but with no measurable improvement. For a long time we had been crying out to God for answers for people like them. After all, if the body is a natural healer, why wasn't the body healing itself?

It's obvious that the body does heal itself of many things, especially in the case of physical injuries to an otherwise healthy body. For example, when cutting up a salmon I had just caught for the evening meal, the very sharp knife I was using slipped and cut deep into the top of my thumb. It should have been stitched up, but I was too far away from a hospital at the time. There was blood everywhere until the deep wound was closed over and taped up. But then my body gotten to work on healing itself. Today there is no evidence whatsoever that the thumb ever suffered such an injury. Within a few weeks it was completely healed.

The body is, indeed, an amazing healer. We all, from time to time, suffer minor injuries and in most cases the subsequent healing is so complete that we never even remember what happened to us. So why isn't physical healing of injuries always like that? Why are there some injuries that heal completely and others that don't? As a scientist by training, I always wanted to know what was going on and I was used to asking the awkward questions – even of God! If you don't ask questions you never get answers.

In our journey of understanding, there have been many occasions when the answers to our questions have not come directly. And when the answer has finally come, it has often been in circumstances when we were least expecting it, such as ten-pin bowling!

I had just put on my soft bowling shoes and was rather casually, with a show of fatherly bravado, tossing the heavy ball from one hand to the other. Suddenly, it slipped between my hands, fell to the ground and landed fairly and squarely on my left big toe! Not only did my toe take a direct hit, so did my pride! It was excruciatingly painful, but I wasn't going to be beaten and managed to complete the game with a rare win over my son! By one o'clock in the morning, however, the pain was so great that I could stand it no longer, and assuming I'd probably broken the toe, I went down to the local hospital and presented myself at the Accident and Emergency desk.

The duty nurse looked up at me as I leant over the counter. I looked down at the pad on which she was beginning to write my details. After my name and address she wanted to know my religion – so they would know which chaplain to send for if things gotten really bad – and then she asked me for the details of my injury. I told her that I had dropped a ten-pin bowling ball on my left big toe. I'm not sure whether nurses are trained not to laugh at the predicament of their patients, but if they are, it didn't work on that occasion! She broke out into a broad grin, as she imagined what might have happened, and then she wrote down in the appropriate space, "Trauma of the big toe."

I leant over the counter, pointed at her upside-down writing, and said, "You've gotten that wrong – I think my big toe's broken – but the trauma's here" as I pointed to my heart! Medically, she was, of course, absolutely right. Any injury to a physical organ is referred to as a trauma. The flesh was bruised, the bone was broken and my big toe was physically traumatized. As I thought about what the nurse had written down, and what I felt on the inside, I realized that there was a disconnect between the physical (medical) understanding of trauma and the spiritual realities. I was thinking my feelings were traumatized by the experience, whereas the nurse only saw that my toe was traumatized.

In reality both I and the nurse were correct. I was feeling the trauma on the inside, while my bruised and broken toe was feeling the trauma on the outside. Every part of my inner being was traumatized, albeit in a relatively minor way compared with the terrible traumas that many of the people we have prayed for have gone through. This was a very minor injury, but it was one that God used to draw my attention to the significance of the inner being, when praying for those who are suffering the long-term consequences of accidents and traumas – especially if the injuries are serious.

I had something very important to think about as I waited for the X-ray which would prove that my toe was indeed broken. The medical fact was that my big toe, and only my big toe, was traumatized, but my toe did not have the accident independently from the rest of my being. All of me had the accident and experienced the trauma, not just the big toe. My feelings were not restricted to my big toe, in fact I am not aware that my big toe had any feelings at all, other than the actual pain which right then was excruciating. But I felt the emotional pain in the core of my being, not in my big toe.

As I hobbled around for the next few days, I went out of my way to protect that toe from any further damage. I was very protective of that particular area of my body as the natural healing process took place and today I think nothing of it, but I am sensibly more careful how I handle the ball when I go ten-pin bowling!

But what if the damage to my inner being had been more serious? How would I have handled it if my inner being had remained unhealed? Could my future life be affected by that hidden inner trauma? I began to think of people I knew whose way of life was at least partially controlled by the consequences of things that had happened to them in the past, especially by irrational fear, even though there was no logical reason for their current behaviour.

Those few hours in the Accident and Emergency Department of Lancaster Hospital helped me to understand that whenever we have an accident that injures the body, it isn't just the body that is traumatized. Our inner being also has the accident and can be suffering just as much as the body – and for a very long time. But what do I really mean by our 'inner being'?

Understanding Spirit, Soul and Body

In 1 Thessalonians 5:23 Paul refers to the whole of man as being spirit, soul and body when he prays, *"May your whole spirit, soul and body be kept blameless at the coming of our Lord Jesus Christ."* So let's unpack this a little.

THE SPIRIT

When Jesus said to the woman at the well (John 4:24) that *"God is Spirit, and those who worship Him must worship Him in spirit and truth"* (MEV), He was not only speaking revelatory truth to her, He was also illustrating that it is with the spirit that we are able to relate intimately, through worship, with God our Father. If God is spirit, and we are made in the image and likeness of God, then the spirit must be the primary component of who and what we are. It is through the spirit that God speaks with and relates to mankind. And it is through our spirit that we can really connect spiritually with each other also.

The spirit is an essential part of our being. It gives life to the body. James tells us that *"the body without the spirit is dead"* (James 2:26). It is the real you, the eternal you, unaffected by time. Your spirit is eternal; when we die our bodies may turn to dust, but our spirit returns to God (Ecclesiastes 12:7).

God's intention was that our spirit should be in constant communion with the Holy Spirit, and that in this way God's Spirit, through our human spirit, can be in the driving seat of our lives (Galatians 5:16–18)

THE BODY

It is abundantly obvious, however, that men and women are not just spiritual beings. For that is what Hebrews 1:14 tells us the angels are *"ministering spirits sent to serve those who are receiving salvation . . ."* As physical beings our bodies are very firmly anchored to Planet Earth by gravity. And our bodies do not have an independent will of their own, they are very much under the control of the person that we are, usually referred to in Scripture as the soul of man.

THE SOUL

It is generally understood that the soul consists of our mind, with which we think, our emotions, with which we feel and react, and our will, with which we make decisions. These influence and, indeed, control the decision-making processes of our lives.

The Bible refers to those decisions that fall outside the plans and purposes of God for our lives as sin. When the human spirit is being led by the Holy Spirit and the soul also chooses to be under the authority of the person's human spirit, then the body will only be asked to do things by the soul that are in line with the will and purposes of God. It is in this place that we have real peace, a peace that the Bible describes as being beyond understanding (Philippians 4:7). And it is the peace of God in our heart that is the most powerful and effective way through which God guides and directs His children.

It is through the soul that we express the unique personality and character that God has given us. When the soul is subject to the headship of the spirit and then to God the Holy Spirit, the character of the person grows and develops in a godly way and the fruit of the Spirit, which Paul talks about in Galatians 5:22–23, becomes evident in our soul and through our behaviour and relationships – love, joy, peace, patience, kindness, goodness, faithfulness, gentleness and self-control.

When the Bible talks about the flesh, it is generally referring to the soul and the body operating together. For example, Paul talks about the sins of the flesh (Galatians 5:19). By this he doesn't mean sins that are committed by the body independently of the soul and the spirit, but sins which the soul chooses to commit and then uses the body to carry them out. As such, the soul is sitting in the driving seat and uses the body like a machine to carry out its desires – either godly ones or ungodly ones.

THE HEART

The soul and the spirit of man are the non-physical dimensions to our being and this non-physical component to mankind is often referred to in Scripture as the heart of man, referring to the way our spirit and our soul operate together to direct our lives. It is the decisions that we make in our heart that determine the direction through life in which we travel – both spiritually and physically.

In Psalm 103:1 we hear the psalmist saying, *"Bless the LORD, O my soul, and all that is within me, bless his holy name"* (Psalm 103:1, ESV). Who is speaking here to the soul? It can only be the spirit of the psalmist, addressing his own soul and telling everything that is within him to bless and praise God's holy name. When our soul comes fully into line with our spirit, like this, in the worship of God, we are then in the place of greatest personal, potential blessing from God. Our heart, both our spirit and our soul, is then in tune with Him.

With this understanding in place we can now move on to look at what actually can happen when we have accidents and suffer shock and trauma as a result.

What Can Happen When We Have an Accident

I still have hundreds of questions about healing for which I'm waiting on God for answers, but in respect of accidents He has already given us some very important answers to our questions. These have resulted in many hundreds of people around the world taking huge steps forward in their physical healing – from consequences as wide-ranging as severe car crashes, falling off cliffs, being thrown from a horse, and being gored by a buffalo in Africa. They found healing and so can you!

You cannot prepare for an accident. By definition, an accident is something that takes you by surprise and which occurs suddenly. Circumstances unexpectedly get out of control and the rest of life's agendas have to be put on hold. In an accident your whole body, or some part of your body, is catapulted into a very unwelcome and, often, damaging painful experience. It is in a state of shock.

Some accidents are extremely serious, causing life-changing injuries and, tragically, some are fatal. But the majority of accidents that people experience are, fortunately, relatively minor. We usually recover fairly quickly, without there being any serious physical consequences. But the circumstances of all accidents, even those which cause relatively minor injuries, can be such that unresolved pain and long-term consequences don't seem to heal. Those who fall into this category form a significant percentage of the people we pray for. It was while praying for a very traumatized person that we were able to take a major step forward in our understanding.

This very significant experience occurred while we were praying for someone whose life had become like my old Alvis car – an almost total 'wreck.' This particular lady had suffered greatly within the cruel confines of a very abusive upbringing and had had all kinds of traumatic situations equivalent to many accidents, and her experience helped us understand what can happen to people when they are faced with seriously traumatic situations.

There were many things we learned as we ministered to her, but there came a time when, even though she was young middle-aged, she was behaving like a little girl. Her behaviour was so convincingly that of a young girl, with all the mannerisms, speech and characteristics of a child, we had to conclude that she was either an outstanding drama student or we were faced with a very powerful spirit that needed casting out! But we couldn't cast it out.

We eventually realized that this wasn't a demonic spirit at all, but it was the lady herself, behaving exactly as she had done at the age of twelve – the actual age at which she had suffered one of her greatest traumas. No wonder she seemed to be such a good actress. She wasn't acting! She was just being herself. This was a totally new experience for us. We had never seen anything like this before and were struggling to understand what was going on.

When God first brought this broken twelve-year-old part to the light, she was very frightened and traumatized, but she was clearly part of the lady we were trying to help. She had been totally broken on the inside and this child-part of her being had been left behind, as the rest of her continued to go on growing through life – but now with a depleted personality.

This particular incident graphically illustrated the most severe type of brokenness where the trauma was so awful and the breaking so complete, that the adult person had no knowledge whatsoever of either the event or its consequences. All the lady knew was that she had intermittent bizarre behavioural symptoms of unknown origin, for which she was being treated by a psychiatrist. Her childhood memories were completely separated from her adult memory, locked away in the traumatized child deep on the inside of her being.

Most instances of brokenness that we come across as a result of accidents are much less severe than this example. Both Jim and Lynda were aware of the things that had happened to them in their accidents as traumatic memories. But neither had any idea of how their traumas had caused a measure of breaking on the inside or that this inner brokenness was the cause of their unhealed symptoms.

I sometimes describe these lesser degrees of breaking as being like a crack in a china mug. It is still recognizable as a mug, but the crack means it is limited in its usefulness – a bit like someone who is still able to function to a certain extent in many, and probably most areas of life, but the inner damage means that life has limitations caused by a measure of disability.

This book is not the place to go into an in-depth explanation of everything that can happen to a person when, as in the case of the lady above, their trauma is exacerbated by abusive intent. But let it be sufficient to say that God was using these extreme cases to open our eyes on what was, for us, a very steep learning curve, as He showed us how to bring healing to this lady's brokenness also and to restore His order in her life. Later we will look in more detail at the various degrees and types of brokenness that are most commonly encountered. Another book will be needed to uncover all that God has shown us in ministering to this particular area of need.

We can, however, look at the basic principles that God was teaching us, about what it can mean to be broken-hearted and how to bring healing to those who are still suffering the consequences of inner brokenness caused by accidents and related traumas.

Revelation from Scripture

Throughout the history of the work, we have always been very determined to stay closely within the parameters of Scripture, and when we have encountered something we didn't understand, we have not wished to go down that particular path of apparent revelation until we have had affirmation from Scripture to assure us that we were still on track with God.

What we were seeing in this lady's life was very real, but at first we were struggling to find any reference in Scripture that seemed relevant to what we were experiencing. We had read of other people in other places who had had similar experiences, but we wanted to know for ourselves that what we were seeing really did have support from God's Word. That support eventually came from the place we were least expecting it – not in an obscure reference in one of the minor prophets, but right in the middle of the personal mission statement of Jesus, taken from Isaiah 61:1, where it says: *"He has sent me to bind up the broken-hearted . . ."*

God had us puzzling over what that word 'broken-hearted' actually meant. In modern English, when someone says they are broken-hearted, it generally refers to someone who is distressed over something emotionally very upsetting – such as the ending of a potential love relationship; or, perhaps, the grief that is felt over the death of a friend or, even, a pet. But the impact of the Scripture seemed to be indicating that it was much more than that, so I asked a friend, who was also a Hebrew scholar, to research the original Hebrew word for me and let me know what it really meant.

A few weeks later, he told me that the Hebrew word that is translated 'broken-hearted' is, as in the English, two words put together. The first time the word for 'broken' is used was when Moses came down from Mount Sinai, carrying the tablets of stone on which God had written the Ten Commandments. When he saw that while he'd been away the Children of Israel had built an altar, and were dancing and celebrating as they worshipped a golden calf (Exodus 32), in his anger he *"threw the tablets out of his hands, breaking them to pieces at the foot of the mountain"* (Exodus 32:19).

The stone tablets, which had been made and written on by God Himself were *shattered into separate pieces* at Moses' feet. This is the literal translation of the word that is used both in Exodus to describe the broken tablets of stone and in Isaiah to describe the brokenness of the human heart. The part of the word which is translated 'heart' represents the inner being.

As my friend explained what he had discovered, God was opening my eyes to a profound revelation – that our inner being can be so traumatized by extreme events of life that it can be shattered into separate pieces. And when that happens it's as if something of 'the heart of man' is separated from the main personhood and can be trapped on the inside, frozen in time at the moment the trauma, and subsequent breaking, took place.

Our experience of encountering a child who had been frozen in time at the age of twelve suddenly began to make sense. God was showing us, in a very dramatic way, how she had been broken by the extreme trauma she had suffered and that the inner brokenness had now been exposed by the Lord so He could heal her on the inside. And that's exactly what He did – this lady wasn't just upset about something (broken-hearted as we might say), her heart was truly broken and shattered into separate pieces. Isaiah had precisely recorded what can happen when someone experiences severe trauma and, what is more, that Jesus was coming to heal – even the most broken of the broken-hearted! We were so encouraged as we pressed on in prayer for her complete healing.

We were living in the reality of Holy Spirit revelation, enabling us to understand how God wanted to transform broken lives and start rebuilding the wrecks that were lying shattered on the ground, awaiting God's answer for their situation. I was reminded of the old nursery rhyme:

> Humpty Dumpty sat on a wall,
> Humpty Dumpty had a great fall.
> All the king's horses
> And all the king's men
> Couldn't put Humpty together again.

In my imagination, Humpty Dumpty represented all the broken people in the world who, through the traumas they had experienced, had had a great fall and lay shattered into pieces at the foot of the wall of life. All the king's horses and all the king's men represented all the failed attempts to do God's work in man's way. But outside of God that's just not possible, so I wrote another version of the nursery rhyme that is possible!

> Humpty Dumpty sat on a wall,
> Humpty Dumpty had a great fall.
> So Jesus the King
> And all the King's men
> Said, "We'll put Humpty together again!"

And that's part of the Great Commission that Jesus gave to the church – to participate with God in the restoration of His people (Isaiah 61:4). Those were exciting days as step-by-step God used the workshop manual of the Scriptures to show us how to rebuild broken lives one step at a time.

Trauma Devastation

As I meditated on what we had seen and heard I began to understand how devastating trauma can be and how unhealed trauma limits the capacity of the body to heal itself naturally. The lady above had been the victim of serious abuse, but there were a lot of people in the world who had not been abused in this way, but who were, nevertheless, not healed from the consequences of accidents, traumatic events and, even, the devastation of wartime experiences.

Could it be that if God could heal the broken-heartedness in a person, we would see a massive increase in the incidence of physical healing, especially of symptoms that were related to the traumas they had gone through? I'd long understood that praying for the symptoms to be healed was largely ineffective if the real issues weren't being addressed. But now God was showing us some of those inner issues which did need to be prayed for, and how, so that He could heal the physical symptoms as well.

One of our older counsellors had been a rear gunner in Lancaster bombers during the Second World War. On many occasions he had had to use his machine gun to shoot a German fighter plane out of the sky, otherwise the fighter would have downed the bomber in which he was flying. He was one of the very few rear gunners who survived flying their maximum number of allotted sorties. There was a huge amount of buried pain as he sent young enemy fighter pilots to their death and a massive amount of hidden fear about what would have happened to him if the fighter plane had gotten any closer.

When we prayed with him, his descriptions of what was happening were far too vivid and real to be the distant memories of more than forty years ago. On the inside he was still living in the reality of events that, for him, had only just happened. Part of his inner being had been frozen in time and when the memories came to the surface, they were as fresh as the day they happened.

I was now beginning to make sense of another of his experiences, something that is a very common symptom of people who have suffered major traumas such as car crashes. Very regularly, and probably at some time during most nights, he would suddenly wake up in a cold sweat reliving one of the incidents he had lived through during the war. He would be in a state of fear and panic. I have realized since then that what can happen during our sleep is that those traumatic events and associated emotions that we instinctively break away from, can float to the surface of our mind when we sink into the subconsciousness of sleep. It then feels as though we are reliving those traumatic events as if they have just been experienced – even though, in his case, they actually took place over forty years previously. It's not unusual for such people to wake up screaming as they think they are about to have the car accident, for example, that caused such trauma, even many years previously.

This is exactly what was happening to Frida, who had been buried alive in the genocide in Rwanda. Before she was healed at Ellel Grange, every single night for over ten years she would wake up screaming as the terrible trauma that was locked inside her surfaced in her subconscious dreams. When God healed the inner trauma, her nightmares ceased.

On another occasion I watched as a very old man we were praying for quite suddenly became unaware of us or the church hall surroundings. He was obviously struggling desperately with what was happening around him as he put his hands out in front of him, as if feeling a wall that was trapping him in. Before long we realized that the symptoms we had been praying about were related to experiences in the trenches in the First World War, with shells going off all around him. Sadly, many thousands of people were diagnosed as suffering from 'shell-shock' and had to endure a lifetime of unhealed mental illnesses. This man wasn't acting, the part of him that had been locked in time was undoubtedly shell-shocked and was still suffering the consequences of trench warfare as if it had only just happened.

As we watched, prayed and saw God bring healing to him, in my mind I was thinking about a relative who also came back shell-shocked from the First World War. Tragically, there was no one in those days who could help him and he lived out the rest of his life in a psychiatric institution. I was weeping inside as I remembered my only visit to see him in hospital, with my mum, when I was a child. I can remember now listening to him describing things that he was seeing that no one else could see. People thought he was mad, but I now know he was simply describing things that were real to him, because he had lived through them. If only I could have gone back in time, with the keys God was showing us, and pray for the healing of his traumatized inner being.

So What Actually *is* Trauma?

Throughout this book we have talked freely about 'accident and trauma.' The word 'accident' is easy to understand, but the word 'trauma' is less so. So far, I have referred to trauma as all the feelings associated with the consequence of an event, such as an accident or a major shock. It is this traumatic experience which causes the broken-hearted condition and which can lock people into an unhealed past. But now we need to look a little deeper at what we actually mean by trauma, how it operates and what its consequences can be.

We also need to see how trauma can also be caused by situations other than accidents. The shock associated with non-accidental traumas has the potential to leave behind inner brokenness, which can then be the source of many other problems in a person's life, even vulnerability to sickness and disease.

In order to understand what trauma actually is, and how it affects us, we need to have a very clear understanding of the nature of man and how God put us together in the first place as spirit, soul and body, as I shared in Chapter 2.

Trauma: The Result of an Injury

In Chapter 2 we saw how the nurse who welcomed me to the Accident and Emergency Department described the physical injury to my big toe as a trauma. She wrote down on her patient record 'trauma of the big toe.' Any part of the physical body that has been injured can be said to have been traumatized. The trauma, as such, can be minor or major, ranging from the bruising caused by a minor injury to multiple fractures that can be the result of a major car crash. Our English word 'trauma' is a straightforward transposition into the English language of the Greek word 'trauma,' meaning an injury or a wound.

When it comes to describing the trauma that is caused to the inner being, however, English has a myriad of different, expressive words to describe the many different types of inner trauma that can be experienced through the ups and downs of life:

Emotional wounding; emotional distress; mental distress; anxiety disorders; fearfulness; shock; birth traumas; anguish; and there are a vast range of psychological or psychiatric conditions or disorders which describe the symptoms that have resulted from the many different inner traumas that might have happened in a person's life.

Trauma is not the cause of an injury – but the result of an injury. If you hit your thumb accidentally with a hammer – it is the injury that is the trauma, not the blow with the hammer. If you are involved in a car accident, the collisions taking place are the accident and the injuries you receive, whether to the body or to the inner being or both, are the trauma.

Just as you might put a fresh and comforting dressing on the site of a physical trauma when the injury takes place, you can also ask the Lord to dress the inner wound and take the trauma out of the inner injuries, the damage that was caused to the spirit and the soul through the event.

Without prayer at the time of an accident, or soon after it happened, the trauma can be locked away on the inside, protected by the broken-heartedness. As a result, all the feelings, emotions and pain associated with the incident are frozen in time, but still fresh, like a bag of frozen peas. And more significantly, this unhealed brokenness will act as a constraint on the physical healing of the bodily symptoms.

The body physically reflects the inner pain that is felt on the inside. The part of the soul which has broken away from the core personhood cannot, however, be broken off from its linking to the body – it is still tied to the body which, therefore, continues to express the inner pain as a physical feeling. Naturally this prompts the sufferer to look for medical treatment to aid the process of physical healing, without realizing that the real source of the physical pain is not in the body, but in the soul! Pain is a signal that not everything is well within, but the pain felt by the body can be a reflection of what's happening in the soul and not just have a physical cause.

Because the person in need of healing is separated from the real source of the pain, which lies in the traumatized and broken place inside, prayer for healing is unlikely to succeed. And there is no medication or medical treatment in the whole world that can heal the inner trauma that has been experienced by a broken-hearted man or woman. The medics will always do their best, without realizing what it is they are up against. They will work at treating the unhealed bodily symptoms with everything from physiotherapy, through medication, and even psychiatric treatment or surgery to try to prevent the pain in the body becoming a restriction on living.

One lady I prayed for had a three-year history of severe back pain. She was about to have investigative surgery as everything else had failed to identify the source of her problem. She was asking for prayer that the operation would be a success. But when I asked her if anything stressful had happened in her life at about the time the pain started, she was quick to say, "Oh yes, my mother-in-law came to stay."

Aware that this could be a sensitive area of investigation, and not wanting to exacerbate family relationships, I simply asked how long she had stayed for. Her reply, "Oh, she hasn't gone home yet" spoke volumes!

What I had uncovered was a wealth of inner hurt, pain and family trauma which had felt, to her, as if she was being stabbed in the back by both her mother-in-law and her husband, who seemed oblivious to the emotional dilemma his wife was in every day – especially when his mother interfered with his wife in the parenting of their children.

I asked if she was willing to forgive her husband and her mother-in-law. She was and I simply prayed, asking the Lord to take the trauma out of her inner being. I've never forgotten what happened next as a root of anger and pain, which had been used by the enemy to create a demonic stronghold, manifested itself and from which she was very expressively and dramatically set free. The pain in her back was gone and instead of praying for a successful operation (which she no longer needed) I was able to pray for healing for her traumatized soul. I then gave her some advice as to how to manage the difficult home situation she was in.

In her case, the inner trauma expressed itself physically by causing the pain in her back. But there was absolutely nothing wrong with the back itself. Doctors sometimes describe this sort of pain as being psychosomatic, meaning caused by an interaction between the mind or the emotions and the body. Sadly, on occasions, such psychosomatic symptoms have given the person an unwelcome reputation, as if what they are reporting is attention-seeking and not real. While there may be some situations where this is the case, I believe that in the majority of such cases the undiagnosable aches and pains are caused by some form of inner trauma, and a completely different form of treatment is called for.

How the Spirit, Soul and Body Help and Influence Each Other

We must return now to the fact that we are made in the image and likeness of God, meaning that there are, therefore, three dimensions to our created being – our spirit, our soul and our body (1 Thessalonians 5:23) – just as God is also three Persons in one Being. We have also established that when anything happens to the body, it isn't just the body that experiences it, the spirit and the soul also experience everything that the body does. In normal life, most of the things that our soul asks the body to do are to satisfy the feelings and desires that are resident in the soul and/or the spirit.

For example, when I asked my body to take me out on a Florida beach at 5.30 a.m. in the morning and watch the dawn rising over the Atlantic Ocean, it wasn't so that just my body could enjoy the view, but so that I could look out through the eyes of my body, now correctly positioned on the beach, and enjoy the beauty of the dawn sky. The scene was totally stunning as the sky was being successively lit by the rising orb of gold from below, and then above, the horizon.

As my soul enjoyed the beauty of the scene, my spirit had gotten in on the act as well and from deep within I began to worship and praise the Lord, the Creator of all things, the One who had set the world in its place so that we could enjoy the sheer beauty of His creation. My whole being was then united in the experience – spirit, soul and body. A little later I went to breakfast and allowed my body to meet its needs as together we enjoyed some wonderful American food. We'd had a great morning together – spirit, soul and body! Each thing we did was enjoyed and appreciated by them all.

In a similar but converse way, when our body suffers the shock and pain of a sudden physical trauma, the soul and the spirit are also participants and are also wounded by the experience and can be traumatized. You can't apply dressings, splints or medication to the traumatized inner being, but we do all we can to soften the blow. For example, when a child falls over and Mom says, "Come and let me kiss it better," those words of love and care bring huge comfort to the child at the time. The kiss, however, has absolutely zero effect on the physical pain, but suddenly the pain seems much less, and more tolerable, because of the love that came from Mom with her kiss!

The kiss wasn't doing anything toward healing the body, but it was definitely comforting the soul and making the pain much easier to bear. The inner being would then recover more quickly from the side-effects of the physical trauma, without any long-term consequences. But if at moments like these there was no mom there to provide the love or, even worse, a mom who was there but who poured scorn on the child, then a measure of inner brokenness can be the result, with related long-lasting symptoms.

However, most moms will instinctively do this. The simple act of 'kissing it better' graphically illustrates how important it is that when a physical trauma does occur, every effort should be made to also treat the inner being with loving care and prayer right there and then. Many of our team, who have brought up children within the work and understand this teaching, will testify to the remarkable effectiveness of praying for God to restore inner wholeness, immediately after something contrary has happened. Asking the Lord to heal any inner damage immediately, arising from outer injuries, has meant that there has been little or no long-term consequences of the many accidental things that happen to kids as they grow up.

Just before I started writing this book Isaac, the ten-year old son of one of our team, experienced a nasty double break of both the bones in his forearm, while playing football in the street. As soon as Mom and Dad knew what had happened they prayed for the Lord to take the trauma out of the inner being, even before taking him to hospital to have the bones set and plastered. Isaac made an incredibly quick recovery and was very soon back playing football, without any fear or thinking he must be careful in case it happened again!

None of us likes to experience the unexpected, especially when it results in a painful injury. When accidents do happen, it is usually the physical body that, quite rightly, gets the immediate treatment, so as to limit the consequences of the physical damage that has been caused and, indeed, save life. After that the body, which has been created by God to heal itself, gets on with the job! All that the Accident and Emergency staff at the hospital can do is put the body back into place and wait for God to do the healing! No doctor can make bones grow together across the cracks and breaks they have experienced, or make an open wound heal. This is what God does through the remarkable ability He has placed within the body for natural self-healing to occur.

In an ideal situation, inner trauma would also be treated as soon as possible after an accident has happened. But, in reality, this has not been most people's experience – even for believers. As a result, a very large percentage of the population are carrying around with them the unhealed consequences of earlier accidents, shocks and traumas.

When an accidental trauma happens, the damage, at one end of the scale, can be so slight that it hardly registers as anything to be worried about. Alternatively, at the other end of the scale, the damage can be very serious, such that the adult person can only cope with the pain, and ongoing memories of the injuries they sustained in the accident, by separating from the reality of what happened. This separation enables the person to more easily move on through life, but at the same time it locks the unhealed part of their inner being into a hidden place.

There can be many such instances in life when something like this happens, making it possible for a person to have many such unhealed memories and experiences hidden away in their past – all of which are locked away 'alive' and from deep within can be exerting significant pressure on both the body and on the behaviour and character of the person, as well as their relationships with others. An unhealed past creates an unhealed present and can change many of the behavioural characteristics of a person, robbing them, and others, of the enjoyment of their own God-given real identity.

CHAPTER 5

Stories from the Coalface

As I thought about all the things we were experiencing, the following question kept on coming into my mind: "Is it possible that when broken-heartedness has occurred because of a major trauma, *and* that when we see God heal the broken heart, we will then *also* see some major physical healing take place as a result?" I didn't need to wait long for God to start answering my question. I already knew in my heart what the answer would be. I couldn't wait to find some more people to pray for!

The coalface is the place where things are actually happening – or, in mining terms, the actual spot where the coal is being mined deep underground. In healing terms, it represents the times and the places where God took us deeper into trusting Him for the healing of His people. As we applied the truths that we were finding within the Word of God, we were discovering how God wants to touch those often well-hidden places, deep in the underground of their lives.

Little by little, I began to include teaching about being healed from trauma caused by accidents in my teaching to the students on our longer schools and courses. We saw God do some very wonderful things, healing the consequences of accidents that had taken place many years previously. Watching people run and jump, rejoicing in their new-found freedom, dramatically illustrated what Isaiah had prophesied Jesus would do in Isaiah 61:1 – set the captives free!

More of Jim's Story

In Chapter 1, I very briefly told the story of Jim. He and his wife were on an Ellel school in Canada, when I first began to teach about what God was showing us. I invited people to share their personal stories of accidents they had experienced. One after another, they came forward to tell of the things that had happened to them. In most cases, it was obvious they were still suffering in some way or other from what had happened.

I was truly shocked at the extent of long-term suffering there was in such a small group of believing people – affecting at least a third of those present! If this group was representative of people in the church, then treating the unhealed residual needs of the population at large medically, must be a massive drain on the budgets of all the nations – my mind was working overtime as I began to think it all through!

Jim told us what had happened when that large piece of timber had fallen from the roof of his barn, while he was sitting on his tractor in the farmyard below. He described how when it knocked him off his seat, his knee pushed the tractor into gear, so that when he hit the ground, the tractor was already beginning to move forward, climbing over his back and crushing his shoulder under the weight of the large rear wheel.

It was amazing that he had survived such an accident and was alive to tell the tale. For seventeen years Jim had not been able to move his arm above shoulder height and for years he had been treated for the consequential pain. He had just learned to live with the disability, considering it a minor problem compared with what might have happened on that never-to-be-forgotten day.

We offered to pray for him on the platform as a learning experience for us all. I had no idea what God would do, but I was trusting that He was in charge! Before starting to pray, we looked at whether or not there was anyone Jim needed to forgive. This was a completely new thought for Jim, especially as he realized that he was the one who had left that big piece of timber lying loosely and unsecured on the sloping roof of the barn.

There was only one person Jim needed to forgive – and that was himself! He smiled as he did so, and those watching exchanged knowing glances as they began to think of things that they needed to forgive themselves for as well. Watching what God is doing for others is one of the most powerful ways through which God gets our attention about similar things in our own lives. After Jim had forgiven himself, I then asked the Lord to go to that part of Jim's inner being which would have been traumatized and broken.

Our physical body often acts as a reflector of what we are feeling on the inside. For example, when you see someone with a smiling face, you don't comment on the happy body that God has given them, but you ask them why they are feeling so happy today! The smiling face is the bodily reflection of the inner happiness. Conversely, if you see someone with a very sad face, it is highly likely that they have experienced something very difficult to cope with and their face is reflecting their inner feelings of sadness.

If, then, part of our inner being is traumatized, unhealed and still suffering from an event in the past, then it would not be surprising if the physical body is still manifesting pain and suffering also, reflecting the unhealed injury which is still fresh and unhealed in that broken part of our personhood. While the inner being may be broken-hearted, even shattered into separate pieces, there is only one body, and those broken inner parts are still tied to the physical body. So what one part is feeling on the inside may be separated from the person's normal feelings, but the pain in the one body will be felt by both parts.

This is a critical piece of understanding that explains why there can be residual pain and physical un-healing in the body while the person feels that they have no problem from the past. The reality is that a part of them, which they are largely unaware of, still does have an unhealed problem from the past, but both parts can feel it because both, as it were, share the same body. This is what I believed was happening inside Jim and so I began to pray, asking the Lord to bring a conscious connection for Jim to the broken place caused by the traumatic accident, so that Jesus could heal him on the inside.

There are times, however, when praying for someone in this way, that God surprises us by what He does next. I was expecting that, as I prayed for Jim, God would begin to heal the inner brokenness associated with his shoulder injury, and with order then being restored on the inside, we would be able to pray for the physical healing of the shoulder. While it was clear that God was at work, and things were happening, what transpired was very different from what I had been expecting!

Quite suddenly, Jim, who had been standing next to me on the platform as I prayed for him, collapsed to the ground and was lying facedown on the floor, gasping for breath and sobbing. A wave of shock swept across the people as they wondered what had happened to Jim. I had gotten down on my hands and knees and tried to speak with him, but for a while there was nothing I could do but put my arms around him and comfort him, as I listened to the sobs that were coming from very deep within his being.

The sobs, however, were not the sobs of an adult man whose voice had broken, but the uncontrollable sobbing of a child – a very different sound indeed.

Because you never know what you are going to encounter next when you are on a healing adventure with God, you have to be ready for anything! You quickly learn how to be praying at two, or even three levels at the same time! Firstly, in this case, I was praying for Jim in this newly distressed situation. Secondly, I was uttering arrow prayers for help to God – I desperately needed Him to show me what was happening and what to do. And, thirdly, I was very much aware of the people who were watching, as some of them were beginning to realize how much unhealed need there was in their own lives as well. Miraculously God answered prayers on all three fronts at the same time!

As I knelt there on the floor alongside Jim, the story of what had happened to Jim as a child emerged. Between the almost uncontrollable sobs of a little boy, for whom the events of so long ago were as fresh as the day they were frozen in time, I pieced together the story.

Jim had been six years old and it was hay-time on his father's farm. He climbed up on the trailer behind his dad's tractor and had a great ride out into the fields where the bales of hay lay on the ground, waiting to be collected and taken back to the barn for storage. The men picked up the bales and stacked them layer by layer on the trailer. With each fresh layer, Jim climbed higher and higher, until he was sitting on the top of a trailer-load of bales, enjoying the ride back to the farmyard.

Then he realized he couldn't climb down unaided, so his dad stood on the concrete floor of the farmyard and called out to Jim on top of the bales, "Come on, Jim, jump into my arms," just like any normal dad would do. Jim was loving the fun of everything that was happening, took his dad's words at face value and jumped from his high position toward the outstretched arms of his dad, waiting below. But then everything went terribly wrong.

As soon as Jim had committed himself to the jump, his dad deliberately stepped to one side and Jim's chest was crushed as he hit the concrete. For Jim it was a terrible, earth-shattering moment – a moment when his trust in his dad was broken for ever – and he heard his dad saying, "That's your first lesson in life – never trust your relatives."

Words such as these, especially when spoken in moments of trauma and distress, can become like curses on our lives, holding people into the bondage of the moment. That is one of the reasons why forgiveness of those who say such things is so important – it's the only way for the power of the words to be broken so that consequential healing can take place. And if these words are believed, as if they are true, even if they are not, it can open the door for the enemy to hold us into a false belief which is demonically empowered. This is exactly what happened in Jim's case.

As he fell on the concrete, Jim's chest was crushed by the impact and he was having difficulty in breathing. And while no bones had been broken, Jim had been crushed and broken on the inside. His breathing never fully recovered from the trauma of that day, and before very long he was medically diagnosed with asthma. For the rest of his life, from six to fifty-one, he was treated by the medics with whatever was the latest treatment for his debilitating asthma symptoms. Jim couldn't go anywhere without his 'puffer' – it had to be ready for immediate use as soon as possible after the onset of an asthma attack. His was a permanent chronic condition which, in addition to the problem with his shoulder, he had just learned to live with.

Amazingly, he had never linked his permanent asthmatic condition with what had happened when he was six years of age. All the feelings associated with that day were locked away in the broken little boy, with all the pain and emotions of the experience remaining outside the passage of time, as fresh as the day it all happened. But God knew and God hadn't forgotten! So when we began to pray into the trauma in Jim's life caused by his tractor accident, God in His mercy used that moment to bring the hidden, and much deeper, trauma into the light so that Jim could be healed of both problems. Since then we have often seen how God uses one set of circumstances to bring something else that was hidden into the light. While praying for people it is always necessary to be alert to God's hidden agendas!

As I began to pray for Jim as a little boy, all thought of praying into the tractor accident was put on one side, and I had to help the boy Jim, in the simplest way possible, to understand that God wanted to heal him, but that to do so he would also need to forgive his dad for the terrible thing he had done. That wasn't easy, but eventually, in the voice and with the vocabulary of a child, Jim spoke out those precious words of forgiveness.

Immediately things began to change on the inside as two things were happening at the same time. First God was taking the trauma out of all Jim's memories of the occasion, and I was taking authority in the name of Jesus over all the spirits of fear and infirmity that had taken advantage of that moment of extreme vulnerability and breaking. I prayed that God would heal his broken-heartedness according to the promises contained within Isaiah 61:1, and we all watched as God was healing Jim in the only way that would bring permanent healing to both his inner being and to his physical body.

Without that deep inner healing and deliverance the only treatment available to Jim was medication for the external symptoms for the rest of his life. But once the inner being had been healed and restored, there was no reason for the outer symptoms to still be there, they had lost their hold on Jim's body. And then it was that the sobbing ceased and, suddenly, everyone watching could hear Jim crying out in a joyful but totally amazed voice, "I can breathe! I can breathe!"

I will never forget those wonderful words for the rest of my life. We were watching what non-understanding onlookers would say was a physical miracle, but what we were actually seeing was the natural step-by-step consequence of bringing God's order into every area of Jim's life, which does, indeed, have miraculous consequences!

On that night, Jim was completely healed of his lifelong asthmatic condition. Jim had suffered from an inner condition that had caused symptoms which the medics described as asthma. But with his broken heart repaired and the inner being restored, his physical body quickly came into line and his body was completely healed and restored.

Having seen and experienced what God had already done for Jim, we then returned to praying for his damaged shoulder and it wasn't long before God had also healed the further brokenness that had happened when the piece of wood came sliding off the roof, knocking him off his tractor. God restored the physical as well as the inner being and everyone could see the arm being waved in the air that previously couldn't be lifted above shoulder height.

It was a joy to meet up with Jim's wife at a conference, many years later, and to hear her testimony that Jim's healing wasn't a temporary alleviation of symptoms, but that he had, indeed, been permanently healed on both counts. Jim wasn't the only person who received healing that night – it's thrilling to watch faith rise as people see God at work. They then look to God for their own healing, knowing that if God did it for one person He could also do it for them. No wonder Paul said in Romans 15:19 that it was through the *"power of signs and miracles, through the power of the Spirit"* (CJB) that he had been able to accomplish so much in his service for God.

Miracles of Healing

One day I was teaching this material in Eastern Europe. The conference information had specifically said that the event was unsuitable for children, so there were no children or babies present in the conference hall. But, quite suddenly, my teaching was interrupted from the back of the balcony with the loud crying of a baby! Before very long the crying ceased and a very excited young couple were seen hurrying down from the balcony to tell members of our team what had just happened.

When Svetlana was born, her mother had a very difficult delivery and it became necessary for the doctors to drag the baby into the world with a pair of forceps gripping her head. Unfortunately the forceps did permanent damage to the baby's face, which did not heal naturally as Svetlana had gotten older. She had a permanently disfigured appearance which, thankfully, had not prevented her husband from falling in love with her, and vice versa.

At the conference I had not only been teaching about healing from the consequences of accidents and traumas, but had also been praying for people on the platform in much the same way as I had been praying for Jim, as described above. This couple did not, however, just watch what was happening on the platform. Early in the teaching they realized that Svetlana's birth experience was a major trauma in her life and as they listened to the teaching, they were quietly applying it to their own situation.

For example, when it came to forgiveness, they didn't just take note of the teaching, they actually spoke out their forgiveness to the doctors who had inadvertently caused the damage. Svetlana knew that God was doing something on the inside and quite suddenly her husband was no longer sitting next to a calm adult woman, but she was crying like a newborn baby, and expressing the hurt and pain that she had experienced in her traumatic birth. Her husband took her in his arms and consoled her. At the same time he was watching what I was doing on the platform and as I prayed for someone else, he adapted each stage of the praying and applied it to his wife.

Before long the crying ceased. He then prayed for God to take the trauma out of her inner being and to heal the consequences of her birth trauma. As he did so, on the back row of the balcony, they experienced a physical miracle taking place. Not only was Svetlana's inner being healed, but her adult body was then able to come into line with the healing the 'baby' had received. The disfigurement which had been there for all of her life was gone. It was not surprising, therefore, that the young couple came running down from the balcony to tell the team what God had just done!

Wherever I taught about accident and trauma, we were seeing God do extraordinary things in people's lives, healing them of conditions that they had learned to live with, following an incredible variety of different accidents that had taken place in the most extraordinary of ways. One lady, Marion, had formerly been a missionary in East Africa. She heard the teaching, saw God healing people on the school and decided that she had to come out of retirement and go back to the village where she had been working and start praying for people to be healed instead of just teaching them the words of the gospel. While there had been some fruit from her years of service, in reality very few people had come to the Lord and there had been minimal tangible results.

At her own expense, Marion went back to that village for just a few weeks to teach them what she had now learned about healing. And people began to be interested, because healing was something that many of the people desperately needed. It was far easier for them to comprehend the love of Jesus and the truth of the gospel when it was supported with living demonstrations! Some years previously, one of the ladies in the village had been gored by a buffalo. She had survived the experience, but it had left her with long-term unhealed injuries. She asked for prayer and Marion took a huge leap of faith. In front of everyone she began to pray for this lady in the same way as she had seen people being healed on her nine-week Ellel training school.

The result was dramatic as God healed the woman of the inner trauma that was locked into her broken heart, and then healed her broken body. Such was the impact of God's healing that at the end of those few weeks, the local witchdoctor came to Christ and they had a public burning of all his regalia and witchcraft artefacts. God was not only working physical miracles, but when the witchdoctor came to Christ the rest of the village were no longer in fear of him, and most of the village turned to Christ also! God is constantly surprising us with what He does. Marion wrote a letter telling me of her experiences and it was thrilling to meet up with her later and hear her first-hand account of all that God had done.

The 'Bus Accident'

The 'bus accident' is an accident that never happened! But it could easily have done and God has used this fictitious event all over the world to illustrate dramatically what happens when people have an accident. It has opened the eyes of those who may have difficulty in following the words of the teaching, but have no difficulty in understanding what they see.

I was preparing the material for our first major teaching tour in Australia. We had been invited to Australia by Dr. John Ouw, a member of a Christian medical association in Australia called Health Care in Christ. While practising psychiatric medicine in Melbourne, Victoria, John had experienced many things in his psychiatric consultancy that challenged his spiritual understandings, his medical knowledge and his experience. There were things he saw in his patients which clearly had a spiritual root, but which he had no facility to treat, other than with conventional psychiatric drugs. He was looking for answers beyond the parameters of his previous medical training. He was no longer content with simply offering medication for conditions that appeared not to be medical in their origin.

In his search for answers, John came across my book *Healing Through Deliverance*, in which I set out the biblical basis for the healing and deliverance ministries as being a credible and normal part of Christian ministry. Deliverance, of course, was integral to the ministry of Jesus. In Capernaum, He delivered and healed a man who had a spirit which made him shout out against who Jesus was, and what He was teaching (Luke 4:31–37). There are many other instances in the Gospel accounts of Jesus setting the captives free through deliverance and bringing major healing into their lives.

The stories of the woman with the spirit of infirmity, who had been bent double for eighteen years (Luke 13:10–17), and the man from Gadara (Luke 8:26–39), whose condition today would be described by doctors using psychiatric terminology, exemplified this aspect of Jesus' ministry. Both were completely healed and restored by Jesus through the ministry of deliverance. And it is clear from the text that something must have happened eighteen years previously in the woman's life to give a spirit of infirmity access to her body. While the Scripture is non-specific, this could, of course, have been through the trauma caused by an accident.

When John Ouw read *Healing Through Deliverance*, he realized that the book contained a variety of possible answers for some of the patients he was seeking to help in his private practice. So, as a key member of Health Care in Christ, John proposed to Ken Curry, the director of the organisation, that the Ellel team should be invited to Australia to teach Health Care in Christ about our healing experiences. The result was a public conference in Melbourne called Jesus Frees, followed by a special private conference, for medical professionals only, at the Merroo Centre, near Sydney. Listening to the teaching would be representatives from all the different medical and nursing professions.

To say I was nervous was an understatement! And as I prepared for the trip and, in particular, the session at Melbourne on Accident and Trauma, I began to think of how I could teach the material in a way that would help people quickly understand the principles God had been showing us. A fictitious 'bus accident' was the result of my thinking.

I invited three members of the audience to come and help me with the demonstration – but I had failed to warn any of them in advance what I was going to do. In real life, people have no idea in advance that they are going to have an accident. And this was experimental, on the job, development of the teaching! Each of the three was to represent a different part of a human being as referred to by Paul in 1 Thessalonians 5:23. The first represented the spirit of man, the second the soul of man and the third the body of man. I asked them to hold hands, demonstrating that the three of them represented the three different dimensions of one unified human being.

I then told a story of how this 'young man' was standing on the sidewalk of a road and his soul became distracted by a pretty girl he had seen on the opposite side of the road, which prompted the soul to tell the body to step out and cross the road, without even checking to see if the road was clear. Because he was distracted by the girl across the road, he didn't see that there was a bus coming – which, in the drama, was me! As the three of them stepped out to cross the road as one person, being dragged across the road by the lustful desire of the soul, the bus barged into them, pushing all three of them to the floor in a scrambled heap. The consequences of the 'bus accident' were lying at the feet of 'the bus.'

A few seconds later, a pre-prepared member of the team arrived, making suitable emergency siren noises as he ran down the aisle, jumped out of his 'ambulance' and began to attend to 'the body,' completely ignoring the presence of the spirit and the soul, even though they, too, were lying in the road, having been felled by the bus in the accident. The body was carried away to the hospital, dragging the spirit and soul along for the ride!

As the drama continued, 'in the hospital,' the doctors also completely ignored the injured spirit and the soul, doing everything they could to treat the body – but only the body. Everyone could see what was happening. In the next act of the drama, after being discharged from hospital, the injured man was trying to do his physiotherapy exercises while dragging around with him, on the ground, the still untreated spirit and soul.

The final act of the drama showed what happened 'years later' when the man was still limping along, and went to the Melbourne Ellel Conference. This time all the attention was given to the still broken inner man (the spirit and the soul). The soul had to repent of being diverted by the pretty girl in an ungodly way, and telling the body to take them all across the road without thinking of the possible consequences. Then I 'prayed for' the injured soul and spirit and saw them able to stand up again, healed. When they were healed, the body also was healed, and the whole person was then able to walk and dance together in unison as one restored human being.

As people watched the drama unfold, lights went on in everyone's thinking. They could see how important it was to treat the body that had been injured in the accident, but how crazy it was to only treat the body, when the whole person had suffered in the accident. And many of the people realized that the drama not only gave them understanding of other people, but was also illustrating something that had happened in their own life, which still needed healing. They were, literally, still heartbroken!

I then asked the people to put their hand up if they now knew that they, also, needed prayer. One of the many who raised their hand was the man who had played the body, in the drama on the stage. When I asked him what his accident had been, there was much sympathetic laughter when he said that he had fallen off a bus as a child! He had not only played a part in the 'bus accident drama,' but was also suffering the consequences of one! God does, indeed, have a sense of humor and it soon became clear that God also wanted to heal the man of the real long-term physical injuries that had taken place at least fifty years ago. His name was Karel – a Dutchman who had emigrated to Australia with his parents when he was only six months old.

My experience in praying for Karel was very similar to my experience in praying for Jim in Canada. The first thing I started praying for wasn't the first thing that God healed. Karel had fallen off the back of a moving bus when a young teenager and had landed with his head on the tarmac. He recovered from his injury, but his neck and upper spine had been permanently damaged when his head hit the ground, and he had walked with an unavoidable stoop ever since. We have found that people who suffer head injuries seem to be especially vulnerable to inner brokenness caused by the trauma to the head.

I started to pray for the brokenness caused by Karel's bus accident, but instead of being able to pray for his heart that was broken at that time, I was suddenly confronted with a man collapsing on the ground, pulling up his legs in a foetal position and sucking his thumb! This was not what I, or anyone else, was expecting. God was treating the people to a further dramatic illustration of how trauma can lock something of a person's inner being into a frozen moment of time. Clearly something serious must have happened when Karel was a baby to have caused this measure of inner brokenness. I had no idea what that could be and 'the baby' was incapable of telling me!

So I asked the Lord to help Karel come back to his adult senses and tell me what might have happened to him as a baby. All he knew was that, on board ship *en route* from Holland, he had caught something very infectious which affected his breathing, and he was completely separated from his mother and put in an isolation unit on the ship for the whole of the long voyage. The distress caused by being suddenly deprived of maternal contact is huge for a tiny baby. While there was no physical injury, we were beginning to understand that non-physical traumas can be as damaging as physical ones and, in some circumstances, even more so.

As I began to pray again for Karel, he returned to the foetal position, sucking his thumb, and I simply prayed forgiveness on behalf of the baby to those who had, for very good reasons, taken him away from his mom, and therefore been the cause of the baby's inner suffering. I took authority in the name of Jesus over spirits of infirmity that were tied to the lungs and asked the Lord to restore his broken heart and bring the broken baby part of Karel to full maturity. I also asked God to heal anything that Karel was still suffering from physically as a result of the trauma he had experienced as a baby. I had no idea, when I prayed, that Karel had been on medication for an asthmatic condition that had affected his breathing as a child and then for all his adult life, and for which he was still being treated.

In much the same way as had happened to Jim in Canada, Karel's adult physical lung condition was completely healed when that inner broken and unhealed part of Karel, which was also tied to Karel's adult body, was healed. When his broken heart was healed, his body had gotten healed as well! Karel went home that night breathing freely, without medical assistance, for the first time.

But he not only went home breathing differently, his neck and upper back were physically healed as well. After we had prayed for 'the baby' I went on to pray for what had happened when he had fallen off the bus as a child. That, too, was a major trauma and we all watched as Karel forgave himself for being in a place of danger and we saw God bring healing to this area of brokenness as well. God then healed him physically and he no longer stooped!

When the following morning Karel gave his testimony to the whole conference, he had everyone laughing when he told them that as he walked home with his wife, he did what he usually did and put his arm around what he thought was her shoulder. But, without realizing what he was doing, his arm actually hit her on the back of the head, instead of being on a level with her shoulders as was usual. The reason? With the stoop gone, he was now two and a half inches (about 7cm) taller than he had been before the meeting!

It was no surprise that many more people came forward for prayer that evening. The team worked long into the night praying with all those who needed help. We had some very interesting conversations with John Ouw, our psychiatrist friend, the following day – he had a lot of questions to ask!

Lynda's Healing Experience

After Melbourne, we headed for Sydney for the private conference with Christian medics. Even though we had seen God do wonderful things at Melbourne, I was still very nervous about speaking to so many medical professionals. This was definitely a new experience. Having found the 'bus accident' teaching so effective at Melbourne in getting a very profound message across very simply, I decided to use it again at Merroo to illustrate the teaching to the medics.

It was after this demonstration, as described in the first chapter of the book, that Lynda, very nervously, came forward for us to pray for her. In view of the setting among so many different medics – ranging from general practitioners to pain consultants, from nurses to psychiatrists and almost every other medical speciality you could think of – I decided to not only pray for her, but to teach my way through the ministry as well. So it was not only a time of prayer for her healing, but was also a wonderful opportunity to take the ministry slowly, step by step, teaching the principles of inner healing, deliverance and physical healing to all those present, at every stage.

For example, forgiving the youth leader was a big issue for Lynda. The group was underequipped with provisions like torches for their night hike in the Blue Mountains. Then during the hike, instead of the leaders keeping them all together, they allowed the group to get broken up. This then had caused Lynda, and the three others she was with, to go on an extremely dangerous route near the cliff edge. They had not been warned of the danger of stepping off the path they were on.

For the past three years, Lynda's life had been totally ruined by what had happened when she fell off the cliff. The only prospect she could look forward to was a lifetime of painful, lonely disability, so forgiving the leader wasn't easy, but we couldn't move forward until Lynda had, of her own volition, chosen to do it. It was almost as though God's anointing for healing was withdrawn while she made her decision. This had to be her choice – not as a result of anyone's persuasion. But once she had forgiven him, the anointing returned and the ministry flowed forwards once again, until we reached that point described in Chapter 1, when we all stood back and simply watched God supernaturally heal her broken body.

Lynda's healing was an undoubted miracle. Twenty years have passed since we watched God at work, restoring her broken life. But shortly after her healing, Lynda had to face one of the biggest challenges of her life. She had previously gone through the process with the Australian Social Security system of being assessed to receive a Disability Support Pension. The doctors determined she would not be able to work to a full-time capacity again due to her back pain and fatigue. As a result she was awarded, and was already receiving, her lifetime disability pension. But now she didn't need it!

She knew in her heart that if she didn't need the pension it would be wrong to keep on taking the money, but it was a huge temptation. She was unemployed and to keep on taking the money would have been a huge financial benefit for her, but she knew also it would have been deception. She sensed that if she did keep on taking the pension, she would have put herself back under the enemy's control and could, perhaps, even lose her healing. She knew that she had to be totally honest before God and man, give up the pension and trust God that she would be able to work and that He would find her a job.

But giving up the pension wasn't as easy as it sounds. People rarely, if ever, cancelled a Disability Support Pension. But knowing Jesus had healed her, and in obedience to God telling her to stop receiving the pension, she persisted. The government office she went to was so shocked when she said she wanted to cancel the pension they did not know how to handle it. Reluctantly they processed the paperwork.

Lynda's own doctor was delighted to validate her healing and record the change in her physical capacities. Then the true litmus test of her healing was that she was able to start working full-time hours again in nursing, including all the manual lifting that nursing requires. She was indeed healed by God, and what Isaiah had said so many years ago, about healing the broken-hearted was, indeed, true.

There can't be anyone whose healing was more witnessed to and validated or who was, therefore, more qualified to have written the Foreword to this book! Her own story, as written in her book, *Lynda: From Accident and Trauma to Healing and Wholeness* (published by Sovereign World) is a very honest account of her amazing journey of faith, including her return to work, falling in love, subsequent marriage, personal tragedy and raising a wonderful family. God truly is a great Redeemer and Restorer of the broken-hearted.

Since then we have taught this material (and performed the 'bus accident' drama!) on every continent and seen God bring wonderful healing to many, many people – not just from the trauma caused by accidents but sometimes by things that had been done deliberately. On occasions we have also had to bring healing to people from the consequences of medical treatments that inadvertently had had very traumatic and damaging side-effects, causing broken-heartedness.

On one occasion we were asked to pray with a lady who was about to pay a lot of money to have investigative invasive chest surgery. She had had a lifetime of severe chest pain. Medically there was nothing further that the doctors could offer and she was about to pay for a private operation to see if the matter could be resolved through surgery. When we asked if she knew of anything that could have happened to her when she was young that had caused her traumatic pain, she immediately began to tell of what had happened when, aged seven, she had developed pneumonia and fluid was building up dangerously in her lungs. It was vital for her survival that this fluid should be removed immediately.

The way this was done was with wide bore needles being inserted through the chest wall into the lungs, so that the fluid could be sucked out with a syringe. This had become a medical emergency and no anesthetic was available, so the doctor had no choice but to carry out the procedure without anesthetic, causing the little girl excruciating traumatic pain. The pain was more than she could stand and her inner being snapped on the inside, locking all the pain of the moment into her newly broken heart. The procedure was successful, but it had left her broken on the inside – until the day, well over fifty years later, when she asked for prayer before her proposed operation.

That hurting and broken place inside was not cut off from her body, however. And the body continued to manifest the pain and be felt by the lady for the rest of her life. We encouraged her to forgive the medics for what they had done, even though it had been with good intent. We asked God to take the trauma out of the broken place inside where she had endured the pain as a little girl, to heal her broken heart and to re-join the broken place to the rest of her inner being. The whole prayer time only took a few minutes, but in those precious few minutes the reason for a lifetime of pain was resolved, the lady was healed and the need for the operation was removed.

Through many such experiences we were learning that trauma doesn't just have to be caused by an accident to leave the person with long-term unhealed symptoms.

How and Why Inner Brokenness Occurs

It is now clear that when the Scriptures talk about someone being broken-hearted it means much more than just being very sad about something that has happened or, perhaps, being in grief over the loss of a loved one. The wording of Scripture is very specific; broken-hearted means an actual fracture having taken place in the inner being. That fracturing can be relatively minor, probably only affecting the mind and the emotions in the soul. Or it can be major, leading on rare occasions to a total separation of the feelings and memories of the broken part from the feelings and memories of the person living everyday life today. So how and why does breaking occur?

The Elastic Limit

The elastic limit of any substance is the limit to which you can stretch it without doing any permanent damage. Once something has been stretched beyond the elastic limit, permanent disfiguring is the result. When a spring is stretched, it will automatically return to its original shape and position after the force expanding the spring has been removed. But if you overstretch a spring, the metal becomes distorted and when you take away the expanding force, the spring does not return to its original length. The metal is said to have been stretched beyond its elastic limit.

A rubber band can be stretched and stretched and stretched, returning to its original size and shape after each stretching, time and time again – but if you stretch it that little bit more, then the rubber will exceed its elastic limit and the rubber band will snap. This concept of the elastic limit is a very helpful way of understanding how, when a person experiences a serious trauma, inner breaking can take place.

Most of us can cope with a reasonable amount of trauma as a result of the resilience that God has built into the human being. We are remarkably adept at coping with all kinds of experiences and pressures. And 'when it's all over' we can return to how we were before the trauma took place, just like the spring, without any permanent consequences. In those circumstances we are operating within the elastic limit of our personhood. But when we are pushed beyond that God-given elastic limit, something can happen on the inside and, like the rubber band, we can snap or, to use the words of Isaiah 61:1, we can be shattered into separate pieces.

Another illustration I find helpful comes from my interest in cars and motoring. The suspension and shock absorbers of a vehicle are designed to take the rough with the smooth. Which means you can pass over all kinds of road surfaces – from smooth to really bumpy and even with some potholes – without any serious interruption to your journey. The shock absorbers take the strain. Each of us has a built-in set of spiritual shock absorbers that enable us to take the ups and downs of life. But if shock absorbers have been running over rough ground for a long period, there can come a time when they suddenly fail and can take no more pressure. We can be like that too. We reach the end of our capacity to cope.

Sometimes, however, the shock absorbers can fail even when in good condition. We can hit something much more serious than a small pothole in the road which takes the shock absorber beyond its capacity to cushion the blow. And that's exactly what can happen to us when something sudden and serious occurs, such as a major accident. We cannot withstand the pressure, our inner shock absorber can't take the excessive strain and inner brokenness is the result.

The actual conditions which will cause breaking are different from person to person. For one person the current rough ground of life may be tolerable. But the same ground for another person who has been struggling with problems for a long time, could push them beyond their breaking point. The old saying "the straw that breaks the camel's back" comes to mind. That one extra thing, in itself, perhaps, something relatively inconsequential, can still be the one extra thing that brings a person to breaking point.

So whether it is something sudden and unexpected, or the result of a build-up of inner pressure over a long period of time, breaking can take place. The broken part of the inner being still carries the source of the pain, but because each part is still joined to the body, the body experiences the pain and the whole person is, therefore, aware of the effects.

This unhealed brokenness, therefore, can cause the person to be feeling pain in the body long after an injury occurred and should have been healed. And it can also have the effect of restricting the activities of a person through the influence of hidden fears associated with the cause of the breaking.

Where is the Elastic Limit?

There is no way of predicting just where the elastic limit is for any one individual. We are all different. Some people have a greater natural strength and resilience as a result of their upbringing and generational inheritance. Some people have already suffered more than most and can, therefore, be more vulnerable to breaking as a result of inbuilt weaknesses in their inner constitution.

On occasions I have been surprised at the extent of trauma that some people have gone through without seeming to have experienced any significant level of inner brokenness. While on other occasions I have been amazed at how easily some people have succumbed to the effects of a relatively minor trauma. There is no rule book, but whatever people have experienced we need to recognize that the whole person has shared the experience, and inner brokenness is always a possibility – especially if there are long-term symptoms which do not appear to be showing any sign of healing.

Physical Events that can Cause Breaking

Here are just some of the things that have happened to people we have prayed for down the years. All of these can be sufficiently traumatic physically for there to have been brokenness on the inside as a result:

Vehicle crashes
Cycling accidents
Boat accidents
Skiing and ice-skating accidents
Swimming accidents
Hobby accidents
Fishing accidents
Air crashes
Falls – down stairs, off walls, off platforms, off horses etc., etc.
Sports injuries
Difficult birth
Caesarean section
Sexual abuse
Rape
Excessive punishment

Parental cruelty
Medical treatments
Dental treatments
Burns and scalds
Gardening accidents
Bites and stings
Violence
Torture
Acts of war
Military experiences and accidents
Etc.

The list of potential traumatic incidents and their consequential injuries is endless and the range of seriousness of injury is equally great. The consequential extent of inner brokenness varies enormously from person to person and can also depend on the age of the person at the time of the incident. The younger a person is when they undergo a serious trauma, the more likely it is that brokenness will occur. Our capacity to handle difficult situations – our elastic limit – increases as we get older. It is for this reason that when young children are abused, brokenness is much more likely to occur than when an adult experiences the same level of abuse.

Young children have very little resilience to cope with unexpected events. They depend heavily for their protection on the covering of their parents, and it doesn't take much for babies and very young children to exceed their elastic limit.

My wife and I were ministering to a man with a lifelong condition. He had been treated continuously by the medics since he was a child, and he had been prayed for many times without any apparent answer to the prayers. As we were praying for him, I was prompted by the Lord to ask him to tell me if he knew anything about his birth experience. He was immediately forthcoming with what he had been told had happened.

His was one of those births where delivery had taken a very long time and suddenly, with the baby partially delivered, the doctors saw that the mother was beginning to bleed badly and her life was in danger. The baby was somewhat hastily yanked into the world and immediately put on one side with no one to attend to him. Only when the necessary work had been done on the mother and she was out of danger did they turn their attention to the crying baby.

But during those few minutes, the baby had experienced a seriously traumatic arrival in the world, followed by the trauma of perceived total rejection at the very moment when he needed immediate welcoming loving care and attention. There was no warm blanket or loving arms to hold him – he was left in a basket to fend for himself during those first crucial minutes of independent life. At that tender age there is virtually no elasticity in the limit of tolerance that a baby can endure and it is not surprising, therefore, that there was both trauma and inner brokenness and that in his isolation and loneliness an unclean spirit of infirmity had taken advantage of the situation.

When we prayed that the Lord would connect the man back to that critical time when he was just a tiny baby, bring the trauma out and then bring a joining on the inside and a wholeness in his innermost being where for so long there had been separation through inner brokenness, we were not surprised to see him experience significant deliverance and then healing of the symptoms that had been a curse on his life for close on forty years.

Non-Physical Shattering

The isolation and rejection experienced by that baby is a good example of a non-physical shattering which is caused through the shock of personal circumstances that have suddenly gone out of control.

I remember praying with a lady who gave me the terrible news that her daughter had died in a house fire. She had returned home to find the house on fire and her daughter was trapped inside and unable to escape. As she told me the story, the details were so fresh in her mind that I assumed this was an event that had only just happened. Only when I asked when the fire took place, and she told me "fourteen years ago," did I fully comprehend how I needed to pray.

She, herself, had suffered no physical injury, but the terrible shock of not being able to do anything about the fact that her daughter was trapped inside the burning house was more than she could cope with. The situation took her way beyond her elastic limit and she snapped on the inside – with all the events of that terrible moment frozen in a moment of time, and fourteen years later, when God brought them to the surface, she was describing an experience that was as fresh as they were on the day of the fire.

Jonathan had spent much of his adult life struggling with psychological symptoms and inner distress which had totally debilitated him and which appeared to get worse as he had gotten older. Neither medication nor prayer seemed to have helped. When we sat down with him and talked through the details of his life, he said in a very matter of fact way that his mother had died when he was young, but his dad had done a good job of bringing him up, and the loss of his mother hadn't unduly affected the rest of his life. He was about to move on to talk about other things, but I stopped him and said, "Tell me about how your mother died and how you heard about her passing."

He then explained that he had gone off to school in the morning and when he came home at the end of the day, it was to discover that his mother had just been killed in a car accident. Not even an adult would be equipped to handle such terrible news without there being some consequence. But for a child it was totally devastating. He snapped on the inside and all the emotional pain, distress and terrible sense of loss were locked away on the inside. As a child Jonathan seemed to have handled the trauma amazingly well; there were few tears and he set about rebuilding his life without Mom in a very pragmatic way.

But deep down inside Jonathan was totally devastated. There was a shattered place inside, broken away and separate, where all the pain of suddenly feeling as though he had been deserted and abandoned by his mother was locked. From here all those feelings became a permanent condition which Jonathan had to live with as an adult, without any understanding of why he felt such inner distress. In everyday life he was extremely competent and able, but his life was becoming dysfunctional because of the emotional wrenching that was constantly going on in the broken part inside.

When God took the trauma out of his fragmented soul, healed his broken heart and released him from the demonic, which had ridden in on his childhood vulnerability, he was healed of the symptoms that were causing him such adult dysfunctionality.

The sudden distress caused by the break-up of a marriage can have a similar effect – especially if the news of an impending divorce comes suddenly, in parallel with information coming to light about a spouse's affair. These are things that are not easily absorbed by the shock absorbers of life.

Here is a list of some of the non-physical things people have told us about which had caused a measure of inner breaking:

Sudden bad news
Death of a close relative
Being present when something bad happens
Watching a terrible tragedy unfold on TV such as 9/11
Professional experiences as an emergency doctor, in the police or ambulance service

Severe rejection
Divorce traumas
Financial disasters
Natural disasters
Bankruptcy
Family feuds
Sibling rivalry
Libel and slander
Public humiliation
Wrong and sinful choices
Failing exams
Being sacked
Unexpected relationship breakdown

Broken-heartedness

What Really Happens on the Inside?

So far in this book I have drawn attention to the fact that there are different degrees of inner brokenness, some being of a relatively minor nature and others being so devastating that the adult person has no memory at all of what might have happened in their past. All that these people may know is that they are struggling with physical, emotional, psychological or psychiatric symptoms for which there is no obvious cause and no clear medical diagnosis. I now want to unpack in a little more detail what can be happening on the inside of people who have suffered different degrees of broken-heartedness.

Understanding the Heart

When we refer to the heart of a matter, most people know exactly what we are referring to – the very core of a situation, the central issue. Whether or not someone's physical heart is still beating is a determinant of whether or not someone's body is still alive. But when the Bible refers to the heart it isn't normally referring to the physical heart, it is referring to the core of our inner being, the very person that we are, the center of our personhood, that which determines the choices we make and the things that we do. You know that if you have a person's heart, you have their full attention, their full cooperation and that you can fully trust them.

That was manifestly not the case with King Saul! For God had asked Samuel to look for another man to replace him as king whom the Lord said would be *"a man after his own heart"* (1 Samuel 13:14). And when Samuel went to the sons of Jesse, the Lord did not prompt Samuel to anoint any of the fine men that were first presented to him, but said to Samuel, *"Do not consider his appearance or his height, for I have rejected him. The LORD does not look at the things man looks at. Man looks at the outward appearance, but the LORD looks on the heart"* (1 Samuel 16:7). And so it was that David, a man after God's own heart, was chosen and anointed as the future king (1 Samuel 16:13).

Within this verse we have an important indication of how to pray for people – we must do as the Lord does – and look on the heart. For it is there that will be found the core issues that become obstacles to healing. David knew exactly how to pray when he came before the Lord for himself: *"Search me, O God, and know my heart; test me and know my anxious thoughts. See if there is any offensive way in me, and lead me in the way everlasting"* (Psalm 139:23–24). David clearly knew that what was in his heart was of enormous significance and he was asking God's help to understand himself.

David was also aware, however, that there were different dimensions to the heart, so that when he prayed, *"Bless the LORD, O my soul"* (Psalm 103:1), he was identifying that the soul had the capacity to be out of line with God and he, the spiritual man, was telling his own inner being to come back in to line with God! Because of the Fall, our soul is very capable of taking us way off course and we can live a 'soulish' life, one in which the desires of the flesh take priority over the things of the spirit. James warned about harbouring *"bitter envy and selfish ambition in your hearts"* (James 3:14) – more evidence of the fact that our inner being can be very polluted.

And in the Proverbs we read the injunction to *"Trust in the* LORD *with all your heart"* (Proverbs 3:5), clearly indicating that it's quite possible not to be trusting *with all* of the heart! It would be very worthwhile spending some time looking up all the references to the heart in the Scriptures. Some of them are very revealing.

There are places in the Scripture where the words 'heart' and 'soul' are used seemingly interchangeably, but the word 'heart' is generally used to describe the whole of the inner being. Sometimes that inner being has become corrupted through the carnal activities of the soul. For example, Jeremiah tells us: *"The heart is deceitful above all things and beyond cure. Who can understand it? I the* LORD *search the heart and examine the mind, to reward a man according to his conduct, according to what his deeds deserve"* (Jeremiah 17:9–10). So here we have Jeremiah recognizing the potential for evil that lies in the heart of man. He also talks about the mind as being part of the heart. Later, in Jeremiah 29:13, we read encouragement from the Lord, *"You will seek me and find me when you seek me with all of your heart."*

One of the many problems I have encountered when praying for people is that they haven't wanted the Lord *with all* of their heart. They have wanted the Lord to heal them, but the truth has so often been that they have wanted to keep control of most of their lives and to keep their own handle on things that they consider to be outside of God's domain!

When you look at all the references to heart and soul and relate these to the practical experience of praying for people to be healed, what becomes clear is that:

1. The heart of man is the core of our inner being.
2. The spirit and the soul are the primary constituents of the heart.

3. When the Bible refers to the heart being broken it is not necessarily a complete splitting of the heart – both spirit and soul. There are degrees of breaking according to the intensity of the trauma experienced, causing varying measures of dysfunctionality.
4. The soul can be out of line with God through sin.
5. The soul can be damaged as a result of trauma.
6. The soul can also be damaged through wrong training and upbringing, which places limitations on the person's understanding

Broken-hearted

So far in this book I have used the word 'broken-hearted' to describe the condition of some of the people whom, Isaiah said, the Sovereign Lord would heal (Isaiah 61:1). 'Broken-hearted' is a very accurate word, describing the condition of those whose hearts have been 'shattered into separate pieces' by the unforeseen events of life. Their hearts are now broken, in pieces, and in need of healing.

The Bible does not use the words 'inner healing' to describe non-physical healing, but 'inner healing' is, nevertheless, an accurate description of the sort of healing that is needed by those who have been broken for whatever reason – either as a result of things that have happened to them or things that they have done which have caused inner damage.

By inner healing we simply mean healing of everything in need of healing that isn't directly physical. Although the truth is that there are many physical symptoms which have a non-physical cause. For example, the woman Jesus healed in Luke 13:10–13, who had been crippled by a spirit for eighteen years, was physically healed when Jesus cast the spirit out of her.

Paul reflects this understanding in 1 Thessalonians 5:23 when he prays that the Thessalonians may be whole in spirit, soul and body. Throughout Scripture there are many places where the physical condition of a person is closely related to their spiritual well-being, such as Proverbs 3:5–8. The Bible does not consider that different parts of our humanity are able to function effectively in isolation from one another. It presupposes that what is happening in any area of a person's being will affect the state of the whole. The stories of the kings of Israel and Judah in the books of Chronicles and Kings provide many such instances where sickness and even national devastation is a consequence of sin and rebellion.

In Psalm 51 David describes his own personal brokenness as a result of his own sin choices. He even refers to his inner being at that time in terms of parts. *"Surely,"* he says, *"you desire truth in the inner parts"* (Psalm 51:6). This is such an accurate description of what can be happening in those broken parts – a lack of truthfulness (dishonesty!) which forms an absolute blockage to the Lord being able to fully heal. It is only when we are totally open and honest with God about all things that He is able to access the inner being and bring His restoration and healing. If we are going to function effectively we need God to touch every area of our being with His healing.

In my days of working on car engines I soon learned that it was no good just lifting the hood and looking at the engine and giving it a clean! If the engine was underperforming it was necessary to find out which part of the engine was dysfunctional and put it right. If one small part of the engine was not operating effectively, such as the carburettor or the distributor, then the whole engine wouldn't run properly. There could be absolutely nothing wrong with the rest of the engine – but until that small part was put right, the car could go nowhere.

This is a very accurate description of how, as believers, we are unable to properly run the race of life if part of our being is unhealed and causing us to limp along in various degrees of dysfunction. Because one part is dysfunctional the whole of our being is, to some measure, dysfunctional also. I have already related Lynda's story. When we first met her there was absolutely nothing wrong with any of her bodily organs or her limbs or her head or her senses! But the unhealed damage in her previously broken spine meant that she couldn't use her legs very well, and the medication for the pain was playing havoc with her internal organs. She felt as though life had passed her by and she was headed for the scrap heap – as has happened to many a good car that only had a minor problem!

Fragmentation

A single English word which means essentially the same as 'being shattered into separate pieces' is 'fragmented' – and the parallel word which means the process of being fragmented is 'fragmentation.' We have found this to be a helpful single word to use as part of our vocabulary of brokenness, to impart understanding of what actually happens when people are broken through trauma. We recognize that there are two types of fragmentation – partial fragmentation and full fragmentation – depending on the extent of damage caused by the trauma.

PARTIAL FRAGMENTATION

It is the soul that most directly links with the body. It is the 'driver' of the machine we call the body. It's not surprising, therefore, that it's the soul, not the spirit, which is the first and primary recipient of trauma in the inner being, following injuries to the physical body. It is the 'shock absorbers' of the soul that take the first impact and strain of whatever it is that has happened. And when the strain on the 'shock absorbers' is more than the person can withstand, the 'elastic limit' is exceeded, and it is the soul that is first fragmented.

As a general rule, in the majority of accidents that take place, it is only the soul that fragments in this way, and not the spirit as well. We generally refer to this type of shattering as partial fragmentation – with only the soul part of the inner being affected.

A lady gave testimony on a recent course to the healing of her back, saying that she could now sit comfortably on a chair, without pain, for the first time in twenty years. Just before giving birth to her child, she had been given an epidural injection in the lower back which, sadly, didn't hit target and caused her sudden excruciating pain. This was a huge shock to her at what was a very vulnerable moment. It did not take much to push her beyond her elastic limit.

She remembered well what had happened, but the pain she experienced had never gone away, even though twenty years had passed. The trauma she experienced caused her to partially fragment and a traumatized part of her soul remained tied to the incident, unhealed and still suffering the pain of that dreadful moment.

After forgiving the doctor who made such a critically painful mistake, one of our team prayed that the Lord would heal her brokenness, restore her soul and set her free. The effect was dramatic and she was completely healed because her broken soul had been healed. Twenty years of suffering was gone in a moment and no more suffering lay ahead of her.

When someone has been partially fragmented, the person has had to continue living everyday life today, split from the fragmented part which broke away in the trauma. They are, however, still very much aware of what is happening when you are praying for God to take the trauma out of the broken part and to heal and restore the inner being. Our general experience has been similar to that which happened with Lynda. Before we prayed she hadn't been aware of the fragmentation that took place when she hit the rocks, after falling off the cliff. But when we began to pray for that broken part of her to be healed, the whole of Lynda was aware of what was happening and was subsequently healed.

FULL FRAGMENTATION

It was a little different, however, when I began to pray for the six-year-old part of Jim, who had suffered the terrible trauma of his father deliberately letting him smash into the concrete. It wasn't an accident, but a deliberate act of cruelty. In some extreme circumstances like this, the consequential fragmentation extends beyond the soul into the spirit. We refer to this depth of inner breaking as full fragmentation. This is a relatively rare condition, which is seldom encountered in cases of fragmentation through accidental circumstances. For full fragmentation to occur there generally has to be some other issue creating an extreme situation that takes the circumstances into a still more serious realm.

Our first encounter with full fragmentation was when ministering to people who had been seriously sexually abused by people they should have been able to trust. Some were severely traumatized as children. Earlier, I referred to our experience of this when we encountered a middle-aged woman behaving exactly like a twelve-year-old girl. I will be tackling ministry to such individuals to a much greater depth in a subsequent book on brokenness.

When full fragmentation does take place, the broken part has its own identity, frozen at the age and in the circumstances of the time when breaking took place. Because children have far less resilience than adults, they have a very low elastic limit. Child parts result from being broken through the deliberately traumatic events they endured, or through very severe accidents or circumstances, especially life-threatening ones, that occurred when they were very young and tender with little resistance to being fragmented.

PERSONPARTS

In full fragmentation, the parts that have broken away are not just separated by splitting in the soul, but by a shattering that has gone so deep that the spirit, also, has been broken. We call such fully fragmented parts of a person's whole being 'personparts.' They have their own separate existence as a fully functioning independent part of the whole person, but are completely isolated from the core personhood. They are locked away, frozen in time, carrying with them all the thoughts, emotions, feelings and pain associated with what happened when they were fragmented off from the whole. They exist outside of the consciousness but, of course, are still tied to the body. They have their own thoughts, emotions and will, and can function spiritually in much the same way as an entire person.

Once they have been fragmented off from the whole, they are out of the consciousness and are no longer subject to the effects of the passing of time. Time, for them, stopped dead at the moment they were fragmented off. They have no subsequent experiences to cause any further change. In full fragmentation the breaking is so complete that, generally, the adult person, who has gone on growing through life, is completely unaware of the existence of the personpart or, amazingly, of the terrible circumstances or damage that they endured much earlier in life that led to the fragmentation taking place.

This is why people can have been seriously sexually abused as children, for example, but as an adult they have no connection to the event having happened. It is only as life progresses, with various symptoms of post-traumatic stress such as panic or anxiety attacks, sometimes chronic fatigue or other physical symptoms occurring, that the real underlying issues begin to have their effect, betraying the depth of inner damage that lies unhealed beneath the surface.

When people are young they have lots of emotional and physical energy, and even though fragmentation may have occurred, they are able to compensate for what's missing, without even realizing what they are doing. But inside what they are achieving is at a huge cost, and as people get older they no longer have the inner resources to handle life in the way they did when they were younger. There can then come a point at which something snaps on the inside and they can no longer hold themselves together. Others notice strange behaviour, some become obsessively compulsive about all kinds of things and begin to manifest strange symptoms, often requiring treatment by a psychologist or a psychiatrist.

The symptoms that are being displayed are not necessarily directly related to the suffering that the fragmented personpart endured, but can be a consequence of what is missing from their life, because part of their inner being is locked in the personpart hiding inside. Their only awareness of the full fragmentation is through symptoms which disable the person from having a normal way of life. Sometimes described as having some form of a breakdown.

Ministering in depth to people who have been fully fragmented through deliberate cruelty and abuse is beyond the scope of this book. But for those who want to be encouraged by reading how God completely healed someone who was fully fragmented and was in a psychiatric hospital when we first began to pray for her, I suggest you get hold of the book *Sarah* by Sarah Shaw and published by Sovereign World. Here Sarah tells her own story of all that God did to restore to her everything that had been lost and give her back her life. It is an amazing story that has brought hope to many thousands who have seen the reality of a restored life, either through reading her book or hearing her speak at Ellel events around the world.

To recap, therefore, in most cases of accident, shock and trauma, the shattering of Isaiah 61:1 can be either partial, a breaking in the soul, or in the relatively rare cases of full fragmentation a breaking of the spirit and the soul.

Dissociation – Self-induced Inner Separation

So far we have been looking at how fragmentation can be caused by external factors, such as an accident, trauma or, in some cases, through deliberate abuse and cruelty. But it is possible for people to develop and use an inner coping mechanism, to help them live with the consequences of inner damage and pain through a subconscious or deliberate process which we call dissociation. Dissociation is a way of coping with things we don't like or don't want in ourselves, so we make a conscious or subconscious choice to push them away. When the choice to do this is subconscious, people are often unaware of what they are doing and will need help to recognize it in themselves!

Dissociation is a choice to chop off painful realities and to continue living in the artificial reality of a newly manufactured persona, separated from the reality of whatever has happened. When praying with people, you can spend a huge amount of time trying to help the now unreal external character without actually touching the truth of what is going on in their lives. The real issues can be disguised and deeply buried behind a series of dissociative choices.

For example, people who work in the emergency services, helping others in their moment of suffering or disaster, can dissociate from what they are seeing and hearing. However, the inner cost of this professionalism in the midst of seeing so much trauma is, in itself, traumatic, and trying to carry on with life without it affecting you can also leave behind a very damaged multiple fragmented inner being.

I once prayed with a former ambulance driver who, as part of his day-to-day work, had been first on the scene at many serious accidents. He had had to separate himself from the reality of seeing other people's lives being torn apart in a moment of time. You cannot un-see things that you have seen, but neither can you live with the things you have seen being constantly before your eyes. In order to cope with the extreme emotional pressures of his job, he simply parked the images in a hidden memory file of all he had seen, along with all his gut-wrenching inner feelings.

That memory file was absolutely full of the most distressing and disturbing memories and a significant part of his personality was being used to keep all that 'stuff' well tied up in a safe place, leaving him to be a progressively dysfunctional adult. It's not possible to do that without robbing your own self of who you are, and as the years go by you lose more and more of yourself to your inner being, and the outer person becomes less and less real.

In time the 'stuff' that is buried, which is not buried 'dead' but very much 'alive,' can begin to force its way into the consciousness and cause significant psychological and, even, psychiatric symptoms which then need to be controlled with medication. In a later chapter we will address the specific issues associated with the military, some of which are similar to those encountered by members of the emergency services.

Conscious dissociation is something that we are all capable of doing from time to time, when circumstances overwhelm us. We have to do something in order to keep functioning as we carry on. But as soon as possible after such an event, it's necessary to regroup and let God heal that inner separation, otherwise the damage will remain locked within. I find it interesting that in recent years the emergency services have begun to employ counsellors who are right there at the scene of a major disaster. Their job it is to care for those who have been at the sharp end of the rescue operation. There is now a recognition in the secular world of what can happen as a result of exposure to excessive traumatic situations. Counseling may help people face what they have experienced, but without real healing the problems are likely to persist.

For some people, however, the process of dissociating becomes a way of life – a means of opting out of responsibilities, not being accountable, a sort of controlled abdication, enabling someone to carry on as if nothing has happened. On the face of it, a dissociate can seem to be an amazing person, who just gets on with life irrespective of the problems they are facing. But often they leave a trail of relationship damage behind them! They just steam ahead like an ocean liner on the high seas, not noticing the little boats that get swamped in the bow wave and leaving everything and everyone else behind. In truth, however, they are living a life of gross unreality, which may seem all right to them, but which causes endless problems for those who have to live and work with them, who never quite know who they are relating to.

In time they learn to exist inside a bubble of a manufactured reality, in which they live and move and have their being, insulated from everyone else around them. They have learned to use dissociation as their personal defence against having to be responsible for the circumstances of their life.

Such extreme dissociation, as a coping mechanism, can often be introduced into that person's life through a real-life trauma, but which then becomes a way of life, providing people with a regular way of escape from day-to-day reality – rather than face the consequences of mistakes they have made, people they have ridden over or sins they have committed, but don't want to own.

Sadly, dissociation can be used to enable people to avoid taking responsibility for their own lives or of taking on a false responsibility for something that is unreal. As a result they can leave behind a trail of confused and, sometimes, very hurt people who can't understand why the person is not owning the reality of what they have done and putting things right. Their friends may be wanting to hold them to account for the past, but they have moved on into a new future and seem to be unconcerned about things that they have chosen to ignore. Dissociation can become a very convenient way of escaping the need for accountability. It is a mask, a false way of living and

coping which needs bringing to the light for God to heal and
restore. Where consequential dissociation has become a
conscious way of life this may have to be dealt with before it is
possible to get to the underlying problem caused by accidental
trauma. Jesus is the way, the truth and the life and it is only in
Him that we can bring the wholeness of truth to our inner
being.

Hope for the Future

The journey God has had us on for these past thirty years is one
that is signposted *hope for the future*. As people learn to trust in
God to heal and restore them, they discover how to leave behind
the grave clothes of pain associated with the traumas they have
experienced in the past.

Jesus is a specialist at not only healing the broken-hearted –
that's one of the reasons why, as Isaiah expressed it, Jesus came
– but also at giving us back our life and enabling us to once again
enter into the destiny that he prepared for each one of us.

The second part of this book spells out the exciting journey
of faith and healing that is laid before each one of us in God's
Word.

Accident, Shock and Trauma: Applying God's Solution

In the first part of this book we examined the problem of inner brokenness caused by accident and trauma and shared many stories of how God has fulfilled the promises of Scripture and brought deep and lasting healing to the broken-hearted. Through the ministry keys that God revealed through his Word, He has transformed the lives of thousands of people.

Our primary definition of healing is *'the restoration of God's order in a person's life.'* Wherever there is disorder, for whatever reason, there are consequences, and some of those consequences can be seriously debilitating, robbing people of the fullness of life that is God's desire for all His people.

One of the things that God taught us in the very early days of the ministry was that if we bypassed the foundations of Christian living and went straight to praying for the healing of symptoms, the person may be blessed by the experience, but it would be unlikely that they would receive the full and long-lasting healing they were looking for.

In the second part of this book, therefore, I want to look at the key steps people need to take in order to restore God's order in their life on the road to healing from the consequences of accidents and trauma.

Building on a
Good Foundation

Medicine, like any other field of human endeavour, operates within the parameters of man's discovered knowledge. It is a godly profession and I thank God for all the blessings I have received as a result. My brother was a doctor and my daughter is a doctor as well. Medicine, however, only operates within the boundaries of the physical, whereas healing transcends those boundaries and speaks right into the non-physical dimensions of what God created us to be – the realms in which physical medicine can play no part.

When it comes to the physical injuries sustained in accidents, all that the doctors can do – and they do it magnificently – is put the body back together as best as they possibly can and then leave the body to heal itself. In these circumstances, doctors don't heal, they simply create the best possible environment to preserve life following an accident and then for natural healing to take place subsequently. That's exactly what the doctors did for Lynda – but when they had done everything they knew, they had to tell Lynda there was nothing more they could do for her body.

At this point, the medical authorities concluded that she would be in a permanent state of injury for the rest of her life and the Australian government put her on a lifetime disability pension, on the basis that she would never be able to work again.

There was nothing wrong with what the doctors did, but all they could do was treat the body. They had no understanding, ability or authority to enter into the province of the inner being.

This is where the medics hit a spiritual brick wall. Where the condition of the body is being affected by injury to the spirit or the soul, or by the presence of an evil spirit, such as the ones Jesus cast out in order to heal people, medicine has no capacity to help with that healing process. All that the doctors can then do is treat the symptoms of pain by medicating with painkillers.

For this reason, when we first met Lynda, she was on heavy doses of painkillers, but the side effects of the painkillers were as big a problem as the consequences of her accident! Without the 'spiritual treatment' which ultimately transformed her inner being, she would have remained in a disordered physical condition for the rest of her life. Her body couldn't be healed until her inner being was healed.

It is, therefore, absolutely vital that we begin our understanding of how to bring God's healing to those who are suffering the consequences of accidents and traumas, by looking at the inter-linking between the spiritual and the physical nature of man. We also need to understand some foundational healing principles that are the absolutely essential stepping stones on a journey to wholeness.

Just as I needed to have a blueprint giving me details of the original chassis design of my Alvis Speed 20, we need to understand the blueprint for humanity that God built into His created order for men and women. Only then can we see where the disorder is and fully understand all that has to be done to put ourselves in the best possible place to receive God's healing, from whatever problem we may have.

A few years ago I wrote an online training program called Ellel 365 (now called *Journey to Freedom*). It was written to help people reach out to God for their own personal transformation, one day at a time. The whole program is aimed at bringing each area of our lives into godly order. Over the years I have been amazed at how many testimonies of healing we have received from people who have taken the journey and who discovered that when they took steps to bring their lives into line with God's will and purposes, problem issues in their lives began to disappear! They received healing for many different things without ever having to be prayed for. God's order always brings His blessing.

God's Desire to Heal

In the early days of the ministry, God brought many people to Ellel Grange for prayer whose stories were far from simple, some of which I have already shared in Part 1. In reality their lives, in human terms, were similar to the remains of my crashed Alvis car – a total wreck. The Alvis could easily have been thrown on the scrap heap, but because, in my mind, I saw the restored and finished vehicle, once again driving along the highway to its full potential, I chose to rescue it from oblivion. My vision for the broken car was like God's vision for broken lives. His heart is never to see anyone thrown on a human scrap heap, but to see them restored and back on the road of life. He wants to rescue them from the oblivion of unhealed hearts and permanently broken lives. How do I know this? Because Jesus, Himself, declared it to be so.

Right at the beginning of His public ministry, Jesus was scheduled to preach the sermon in his home synagogue at Nazareth. He had just returned from a time of fasting in the wilderness, where the devil had been tempting him to give up on His mission before it had even begun. But Jesus resisted all the devil's temptations with quotations from the book of Deuteronomy and, instead of capitulating to the devil's temptations, He returned to Nazareth in the power of the Spirit ready for action (Luke 4:14).

The very first text He chose to speak from was the Messianic prophecy about Himself in Isaiah 61:1. Here the prophet Isaiah said that the Sovereign Lord would preach good news to the poor, heal the broken-hearted, proclaim freedom for captives and release from darkness for prisoners. *"Today,"* Jesus said, *"this scripture is fulfilled in your hearing"* (Luke 4:21). Jesus was the 'Sovereign Lord' Isaiah had been talking about. And here He was openly declaring that He would begin His work just as Isaiah had prophesied, with healing the sick, the hurting and the broken. That was the number one item on His prophetic agenda – it was top of His list of initial priorities. It was an objective that had been spelled out by David in the Psalms as well: *"The LORD is close to the broken-hearted and saves those who are crushed in spirit"* (Psalm 34:18) and *"He heals the broken-hearted and binds up their wounds"* (Psalms 147:3).

This amounted to Jesus firing the first rounds in a spiritual battle for the rescue and restoration of God's people that is still going on today. At the beginning of John's Gospel we read that *"to all who received him, to those who believed in his name, he gave the right to become children of God"* (John 1:12). Throughout His ministry, Jesus never stopped loving and welcoming those who came to Him, healing them, delivering them and setting them free. Even on the cross Jesus was telling the criminal who recognized who He was, and believed, that he would soon be with Him in Paradise!

When Jesus sent His own disciples out to preach and to teach, He also told them to heal the sick and to cast out demons (Luke 9:1–2). And finally, just before Jesus went back to Heaven, He commissioned those first disciples to go into all the world and make more disciples who would keep on doing what the first disciples had been taught to do (Matthew 28:18–20) until He comes again. And here we are today, living out our lives in that gap between Jesus' first and second comings, and the Bible tells us unequivocally that Jesus wants us to come to Him as His children and that He wants to heal and restore us.

I have absolute confidence, therefore, that God loves each one of His children, and also that He wants to heal even the most hurting. It's not for nothing, for example, that one man Jesus chose to heal, who we call the Gadarene demoniac (Luke 8:26–39), was suffering the most extreme of uncontrollable psychiatric symptoms – not even being chained hand and foot and put under guard was enough to restrain him! He was a total wreck, but after Jesus had healed him he was restored and *"in his right mind"* (Luke 8:35). We have no idea what had happened to this man to cause his problems, but whatever it was, the devil had done his best to lock him into an uncontrollable demonic world. But the deliverance and healing Jesus brought was sufficient for all his needs!

Healing is a vital part of the Good News of the gospel. Jesus healed people and He taught His disciples to do the same. So, when some of the most hurting and broken of God's children came to Ellel Grange asking for help, I had no hesitation in beginning to walk with them in faith as they trusted their lives to God and cried out to Him for their healing. We may not have understood all that we were seeking to do in those early days, but God led us to trust in the One who did understand and who wanted us to learn from Him.

The ones through whom we learned the most profound lessons were not those who just wanted a bit of healing so that they would feel better, but those who were looking for God to have His way in every area of their lives, whatever the cost might be of facing the need for uncompromising truth. They weren't just wanting prayer so that they could carry on with their unchanged lifestyles, uninterrupted by their symptoms, but were looking for Jesus the Healer to heal them from the inside out – not the other way around. They wanted healing that would last, not just a temporary experience of the Spirit of God.

It was not an easy journey though. At times, ministering to some of these people was, in mountaineering terms, like climbing Everest! But in climbing Everest you learn much more about overcoming real problems than you would ever learn from a gentle walk in the hills on a Sunday afternoon. God had us on a very steep learning curve of understanding, in order to tease out some very important foundational principles of healing, so that these could then be applied to real issues in the lives of thousands of people, the majority of whom would be less severely damaged.

This process of exploration and learning is part of the normal pattern of discovery in every arena of human endeavour, even in the ministry of healing. Science and technology pioneers may have to do thousands of costly experiments before they make the unique discovery that can change the world for everyone else. For example, we all benefit from using non-stick saucepans, but the people who use them have no desire or need to understand the experimental journey that led to the accidental discovery of the non-stick substance! Similarly, when we switch on a light no one thinks about the thousands of hours of scientific discovery that preceded the invention of the first working light bulb – they just enjoy the light!

It was as we were climbing our own personal Everest that God gave us understanding of the spiritual principles we would later teach all over the world, which would bring hope and healing to thousands of people in all kinds of different situations and condition – including those suffering from the consequences of accidents and trauma. But to fully understand these principles, we need to go right back to the beginning of God's Word.

Healing Foundations

In the book of Genesis we read that each one of us is made in the image and likeness of God (Genesis 1:27). What men and women look like is a reflection of what God looks like. Jesus did not have to contort His being and transform Himself from some other image in order to look like a man. He already looked like a man, because man was created to look like God. Jesus looked like the image of God (2 Corinthians 4:4), therefore, and we look like Him.

And we are like Him in another vital way as well. Just as God is three in One – so are we! God is Father, Son and Holy Spirit and we are spirit, soul and body. And it is these three distinct constituents that define our humanity and set us apart from every other living being. Every human being has a spirit through which we are able to have fellowship and relationship with God, who is also a spiritual being (John 4:24). But we also have a *soul,* in and through which we are able to think with our *mind,* react with our *emotions* and make decisions with our *will.* It is through the soul that we are able to express our unique God-given personality and character. And finally, our spirit and our soul are anchored within our *body,* and as long as they remain anchored in that place we are said to be alive. Our human life begins at conception, and death is defined by the moment when our spirit and our soul leave our body and enter into the timelessness of eternity (Ecclesiastes 12:6–7; James 4:13–14).

God gave man authority to rule over the Earth (Genesis 1:26) and His original intention for mankind was that men and women should not only populate the planet (Genesis 1:28) but also remain in fellowship and covenant relationship with Him. What happened next, however, has determined both the course of history for the human race and the consequential actions of a loving God.

What's generally known as *the Fall of man* took place when man chose to listen to the voice of the tempter and obey Satan. At that moment the whole of the human race came under Satan's authority, and instead of man being in a place of dominionship over the world God had made (Genesis 1:27–30), Satan now took that control into his own hands and became the ruler of the planet (1 John 5:19). Ever since, Satan has been the spiritual authority that has kept sinful man separated from his holy God. All the past, present and future evil in the world originates from man's choice and the authority that Satan was consequentially given as a result of that choice. Satan became the god of this world who has *"blinded the minds of unbelievers, so that they cannot see the light of the gospel of the glory of Christ, who is the image of God"* (2 Corinthians 4:4). John said that *"the whole world is under the control of the evil one"* (1 John 5:19) and Jesus referred to him as *"the prince of this world"* (John 12:31).

Man's rebellion against his Creator is called sin. It is through sin that man became separated from God and that Satan's punishment of eternal death became the inheritance of the human race. From that moment onwards, even though mankind had been made in the image and the likeness of God, the nature of his inner being became fleshly, or carnal, with a propensity to sin as a result. It is always a battle to make godly choices, for our intrinsic carnal nature will fight against what is God's best for us.

The will of man determines what we actually do with our whole being. Other than in the essential bodily functions, such as the beating of the heart and the functionality of all the internal organs, our body does not act independently of our soul and then tell the soul what it has done! It is always the other way around. We are created with the capacity to choose what we do – be it good or evil – and our carnal nature has assumed the driving seat.

At the Fall, man chose the evil of rebellion, and every time we allow our choices to be dictated by the same motivating forces we are allowing the carnal nature to be in charge of the steering wheel of life. When the Bible talks about our need to crucify the flesh, this is exactly what it means – put to death the choices that originate from our carnal nature and choose to walk in righteousness (Romans 6:5–23; Galatians 5:24).

God made us to be either male or female (Genesis 1:27). While all men and all women have a spirit, a soul and a body, men and women have unique gender-defining physical appearances, the body being a reflection of the intrinsic gender characteristics that are also a feature of the spirit and the soul. The sexuality of each human being is present in the spirit and soul at conception and the body develops in line with God's created order. God's ideal for sexual relationships is that they should be the means through which mankind would populate the world (Genesis 1:28) within the covenant of marital relationships. Sexual relationships outside the covenant of marriage are specifically forbidden by God's Ten Commandments (Exodus 20:14), teaching which is reinforced throughout Scripture from beginning to end. Jesus even described unfulfilled lustful desires as adulterous sin because that would be the desire of the heart – and God looks on the heart (1 Samuel 16:7).

While it is of course possible for unmarried men and women to have intercourse together and treat sex as a form of personal recreation, devoid of the responsibilities, provisions and blessings of the covenant of marriage, this was not what God intended. Sexual union within marriage produces a marriage bond that joins husband and wife together in a mystical union of spirit and soul – one way to describe this is as a *soul-tie*. Inside marriage this is a godly soul-tie which is a source of harmony, unity and blessing. Sexual relationships outside of marriage still result in a mystical union between sexual partners, but this time the soul-tie is ungodly. Godly soul-ties are blessed by God, but ungodly ones provide the perfect opportunity for the enemy to enter and control our lives from within.

God does not suspend the outworking (making of soul-ties) of his created order for sexual relationships, so that people can have unrestricted sex without there being any spiritual consequences. Where sexual soul-ties have been made, they remain in place until broken by God. It is He who joins people together through sexual union and it is only He who can 'unjoin' them following real repentance and then healing. Unconfessed sexual sin, and the consequential bondage of ungodly soul-ties, can be a major obstacle to healing, and also be a gateway for the demonic to enter, resulting in the need for deliverance.

There are other forms of soul-tie as well, both godly and ungodly, which do not involve sexual relationships, but which are of an emotional or spiritual nature, or even an outworking of agreements between individuals or organizations.

In summary, we have seen how God designed and created human beings with a spirit, a soul (which embraces our mind, our emotions and our will) and a body (1 Thessalonians 5:23). And the fact is, we can be sick or damaged in any one of these five areas of our being. So when we are praying for healing it can be important to know where the damage is, so that any residual issues (such as unforgiveness) can be resolved, and healing prayer can be specifically targeted at the root of the problem. This is especially important where the body has been affected by damage that has taken place in the spirit or the soul. If the inner damage is unhealed, then the outer healing in the body is often limited.

There are many ways in which we can knowingly, or sometimes unknowingly, transgress God's law. God's law is not a set of rules that He devised to try to keep man in order! God's law is simply the consequence of who God is and who we are. For example, the law of gravity is built into the physical universe – if we drop something it will always fall to the ground as a result. We cannot change the law of gravity, either through prayer or choice, so man in his earthly wisdom does everything he can not to fall foul of the law of gravity, for there will be consequences if he doesn't. So you take special care when you are close to the edge of a high cliff, such as Beachy Head in the south-east of England, or a tall building. You know that if you fall off, serious, or even fatal problems could result.

No one complains about the law of gravity – it is a fact of life and we are grateful when, for example, we read a sign warning us of danger if there is a possibility of us discovering the law of gravity the hard way. In fact, if there wasn't a sign at Beachy Head, warning people of the danger of going too close to the edge of the cliff, they would undoubtedly complain to the authorities!

God, as Creator of the universe, is the ultimate authority and in His mercy He has shown us the key areas of life where, if we ignore what He has said, we will discover the consequences the hard way. The Bible refers to these as the Ten Commandments. They are an expression of God's covenant love (Deuteronomy 4:13) and mercy. Choosing to disobey them is a bit like ignoring the sign at Beachy Head and walking off the edge of a cliff, even though we know about the law of gravity and understand what the result will be. The problem is, most of the world doesn't believe in the relevance of God's law anymore and is walking as if blindfolded toward the edge of a very steep spiritual cliff.

When we choose to disobey God's Word like this, we are stepping outside the provisions of His covenant love. The Scripture is full of warnings of what can happen as a result. For example, Proverbs 3:7–8 says, *"Do not be wise in your own eyes, fear the LORD and shun evil. This will bring health to your body and nourishment to you bones."* The implication is that if we don't avoid evil then there could be consequences that we will have to live with as a result. In fact the second part of Deuteronomy 28 (verses 15–68) gives us plenty of examples of what can happen when we choose to step outside God's parameters of safety as expressed by His covenant of love. This is why James was so specific about the need to deal with our own personal sin as part of the process of coming to God in prayer for any form of healing (James 5:16).

God's rescue plan for mankind was first prophesied in Genesis 3:15. It finally came to fulfillment when Jesus was conceived by the Holy Spirit in Mary and lived and died as a sinless human being to deal with the sins of the world. It was only through the death of a sinless Savior, who was not under the control of the evil one, that there could be any way for us to escape from sharing the same eternal punishment that had been prepared for Satan, for his own rebellion as an angelic being (Matthew 25:41).

It is only through Jesus, who never succumbed to Satan's temptations, that sin can be forgiven and men and women can come out from under the control of the evil one and his intentions. It is through the ongoing practice of sin (rebellion against God, His law and His Word), that all the sickness, disease and traumas of mankind have taken root in humanity. And because Jesus is the only One who has overcome temptation, never sinned and died in a place of sinless victory, He is the only One through whom we can receive forgiveness and through whom true healing can take place.

Earlier we saw how John the Apostle summed up the choice we can make to either receive or reject Jesus. Those who accepted Him (John 1:12) were then born again – not this time as *"children . . . of natural descent, nor of human decision or a husband's will, but born of God"* (John 1:13). It doesn't matter whose choice it was that we were physically born, or even if it would seem we were an accidental consequence of someone else's sinful relationship, what eternally matters is that we are born again – for all those who are born again spiritually, irrespective of the circumstances of their natural birth, all have the same spiritual inheritance – they are brothers and sisters in Christ!

When Isaiah prophesied about the coming of the Sovereign Lord, the Messiah, he stated so clearly that He would come to heal the broken-hearted and set the captives free (Isaiah 61:1). Only He could set us free from the carnal inheritance we received through the Fall and give us a new inheritance in Him. And only He could undo any of the sinful consequences of the sin of mankind. No wonder Satan hated Jesus's healing ministry, for it was dramatic day-by-day evidence of His victory over the evil one and of His authority and power. Then, when Jesus sent the disciples out to heal the sick, He gave them His power and His authority also (Luke 9:1–2). Without that, they were unable to help anyone. But with that, all these blessings could be enjoyed in Christ, first in time and then in Heaven with Him for eternity. *"[E]veryone who believes in him may have eternal life. For God so loved the world that he gave his one and only Son, that whoever believes in him shall not perish but have eternal life"* (John 3:15–16).

It is a fact, also, that we can be hurt, not just by the consequences of the things we do, but as a result of what others do to us – either deliberately or accidentally. Every accident, for example, has a cause. Whenever there is a road traffic accident, the police go to huge lengths to determine exactly what happened as so much hangs, legally and financially, on correctly apportioning blame for the circumstances of the incident.

When we suffer as a result of what someone else has done to us, even if what happened was unintentional, we become a victim, and as a victim we come under the spiritual influence and even control of the perpetrator, which acts like a curse upon us. That is one of the main reasons why there are such long-term consequences of sexual abuse.

When seeking to deal with the things that others have done to us, Jesus only gave us the one remedy. In Luke 6:28 Jesus said, *"bless those who curse you, pray for those who ill-treat you"* and that is not an easy thing to do.

So how do we bless those who have hurt us? The first step is the biggest step of all – but it's the step which unlocks the power and blessing of God. It's forgiveness. This is so important that after He had given us the prayer we call the Lord's Prayer, Jesus said, *"if you do not forgive men their sins, your Father will not forgive your sins"* (Matthew 6:15). How terrible not to be able to receive the Father's forgiveness for the things we have done. If our unforgiveness can act like a shield preventing us from receiving the loving forgiveness of God, then forgiveness has to be a very high item on the agenda of our life, without which we will be causing ourselves untold harm.

The issue of forgiveness is so important, especially in the case of accidents and traumas we may have experienced, that we will spend the whole of the next chapter seeking to understand the importance of this vital issue.

The last foundational principle that I want to emphasize, before we press on with our journey, relates to the work of the enemy in our lives. We saw how the Fall of man came about through man submitting to the temptation of Satan. But Satan is not a solitary spiritual being. Jesus was very clear, on many occasions, that what He was dealing with in the lives of those who came to Him was the presence of one or more evil (unclean) spirits. It's clear from the story that there were probably hundreds of evil spirits in the Gadarene demoniac. And Luke 8:2 tells us about Mary Magdalene *"from whom seven demons had come out . . ."*

There are many different ways through which demons can come into a person. One of these is because of our spiritual vulnerability during times of trauma. For example, a spirit of fear can enter at the moment an accident takes place. Lynda was aware of this happening to her as she fell through the air after falling from the cliff. And Paul was careful to warn the Ephesians not to give a foothold to the enemy (Ephesians 4:27) through any of the many different sinful behaviours he was talking about in his letter. When the ground has been carefully prepared, it is often through deliverance ministry, at the end of a time of healing prayer, that we have sometimes seen the most dramatic and permanent healing take place.

Deliverance can be such an important part of the healing process for those who have been traumatized through an accident that we will be devoting a whole chapter to this topic also.

And so we can now return to our journey of understanding how to pray for people who have suffered the consequences of accidents and traumas – but before we get down to some of the details we need to look again at the subject of forgiveness. Forgiveness is the key that can unlock the most stubborn of doors to healing.

Forgiveness: The Doorway of Hope

When praying for people who are still suffering the consequences of accidents and traumas, one of the first questions I usually ask is "Have you forgiven those who were responsible?" Their response is often very revealing. Some will question whether that really matters now. Others might fly into incandescent anger, furious that I would even dare to suggest that they should forgive the very person who had ruined their life! But, somewhat surprisingly, in view of the depth of pain so many have suffered, the most common answer is "I've never even thought about it!"

Most people are aware that what happened has caused them a lot of pain and heartache, but they have buried the circumstances a long time ago and now they are just focusing on overcoming the residual symptoms. It has never even occurred to the majority of them that there could be any link between today's problems and whether or not they have forgiven anyone who was responsible for hurting them, either deliberately or accidentally.

The pain of past accidents and traumas is generally of two kinds – pain in the heart and pain in the body. Unless we fully deal with the pain in the heart, the unhealed pain in the body is likely to be around for a long time to come, no matter how much we may think we can bury the pain in the heart, and forget about it. If there is an unforgiveness issue surrounding it, the pain will go rotten in the ground of our lives and will still be having a massive effect on whether or not our body is going to be healed.

Because the soul is in the driving seat of the body, what's going on in the soul will, as a result, be influencing what's happening in our body. And ever-present inner anger, bitterness or resentment is an absolute blockage to the possibility of full healing taking place. So many are trapped in a self-inflicted prison that they have created by building walls of unforgiveness around their heart.

In praying with thousands of people over many, many years of ministry, the largest single obstacle I have found to people knowing the healing and restoring power of God is their unforgiveness of those who have hurt them! That is fact – and that being the case, I am trusting that you won't want to skip this chapter. For you, it could be the most important chapter in the book.

Unfortunately, for all kinds of reasons, the carnal nature fights against doing such a thing. But it is worth reiterating from the last chapter that Jesus didn't hesitate to make the forgiveness issue very clear in the Lord's Prayer by linking the forgiveness of our own sins to whether or not we are forgiving other people. Then, as if it wasn't already clear he repeated Himself by saying, *"if you forgive men when they sin against you, your heavenly Father will also forgive you. But if you do not forgive men their sins, your Father will not forgive your sins"* (Matthew 6:14–15). So there you have it, straight from the mouth of Jesus – if you don't forgive others, then God won't forgive you! If we're honest, those are words that none of us really want to hear. For when other people have hurt us, we instinctively rise up in self-defence and justify our reactions with thoughts such as "but what they did to me is far worse than anything I've ever done" or *"they don't deserve to be forgiven!"*

And, unfortunately, that's probably true – they don't deserve to be forgiven! But that doesn't mean we can choose not to forgive. The fact is, neither do you or I deserve to be forgiven! Forgiveness is not a matter of whether we deserve it or not – it's a matter of grace and mercy, motivated by love. I can hear some of you saying something like "But Jesus . . . You don't understand . . . that's so hard!"

It's easy to start arguing with Jesus about having to forgive others! And the arguments can seem so sensible: *"Just look at what they've done to me – why should they get off? Why should I suffer for what they've done and then forgive them as if it doesn't matter? They've ruined my life. It's not fair! Surely, Lord, my situation is much worse than anyone else's. You can't really expect me to forgive after all they've done – can You?"*

But then our mind turns to that scene at Calvary. Jesus, the totally sinless Son of God, is being nailed to a wooden cross for something He's never done, and from His lips come these words, *"Father, forgive them, for they do not know what they are doing"* (Luke 23:34). Our arguments for not forgiving melt away when we think about what He did for us.

Real-life Stories

Some time ago I visited Rwanda, in Central Africa. In 1994 there was a terrible genocide when about a million Tutsi people were massacred by the Hutus. In spite of the terrible traumas of the recent past, it was wonderful to spend time with people from both sides of the conflict, and see how God is rebuilding the nation through forgiveness and reconciliation.

One of the people who suffered greatly in the genocide was a thirteen-year-old girl called Frida, whom I mentioned earlier. All of the rest of her family were killed on the same day and she was buried, still alive, with them all. But, miraculously, she survived the heavy blow to her head that should have killed her and fourteen hours later someone heard a noise coming from the shallow grave and dug her out. Her suffering was terrible.

A few years later she became a Christian and her life was totally transformed. It was then, as she read her Bible, that she understood Jesus was asking her to forgive the people who had done these terrible things. The man who killed her father was now in prison, so she went to the jail to speak forgiveness to him.

It was this act of obedience to Jesus that opened the door for her healing. Twelve years after her ordeal, she came to Ellel Grange on a nine-week training school The trauma she had been through was still tormenting her head, night after night. But when she was prayed for in the way that will unfold through the remaining pages of this book, she was physically healed of the constant head pains and of the nightmares that had been the result of her terrible experience. Forgiveness opened the door to both healing and restoration.

Forgiveness didn't change Frida's history, but it did change her future. It meant that Frida would be able to live the rest of her life without being forever locked in the chains of bondage that unforgiveness can wrap around our hearts. It isn't true to say that Jesus doesn't understand our own situations. He not only understands, but He has walked through the ultimate forgiveness test himself – forgiving those who were taking His own life for something He hadn't done. Jesus helped Frida walk a similar pathway – a journey that she will never regret.

I once prayed with a lady who had been very bitter for thirty years, because of what cruel people had done to her. She had vowed never to forgive them. But the consequence in her life was a steadily deteriorating physical condition that was slowly eating her life away. In just the same way bitterness was eating her heart away.

She came for prayer for her physical condition, but forgiving those who had hurt her was not on her original agenda with God! She was quite angry when I taught her about the need to forgive. But when she finally made the choice to forgive, the power of God was released into her life. First God healed her heart and then she received major physical healing for the condition that had formerly crippled her.

As another example, a lady in Canada was wearing a protective collar around her neck to prevent the possibility of painful jarring of the vertebrae. Many years previously she had been on the back of an ice-bike, traveling at a high speed across a frozen lake. Suddenly the driver lost control and the lady was thrown over the front of the bike, landing on her head and bouncing several times before coming to rest on the ice.

Her injuries were serious and after the doctors had done their best, she was left with a painful spine and the residual damage to her neck. These had restricted her movements for all the rest of her life. She had never been able to ride a bike, carry bags of shopping or even pick up her own children without being in excruciating pain. She was clearly still very broken on the inside, but when we began to pray that the Lord would take out the trauma from her inner being and heal the broken heart, it was if God had gone on holiday and there was no anointing for healing. I then remembered that I hadn't asked her about whether or not she had forgiven the driver of the bike. When I asked the question, the look on her face said it all. She angrily cried out, "He ruined my life!"

We couldn't continue with the prayer ministry until she had gone off with one of our ministry team to gain some understanding of what forgiveness really means, and then done some real business with God about the issue. A couple of hours later she returned and the look on her face was very different. And as soon as we began to pray the presence of the Holy Spirit was very real and we watched as God totally healed her neck.

The following morning she rose early and went for a jog around the grounds – something that would have been totally impossible for her previously. And when her teenage children saw what God had done for her, they were deeply impacted and gave their lives to the Lord. Time and again we have seen how healing and evangelism are inseparable agents of the Kingdom of God. It's no wonder that Jesus began His ministry by proclaiming healing!

The Lord's Prayer

It's clear from the Lord's Prayer that, for followers of Jesus, forgiveness has to be a way of life. But it's not easy and even Simon Peter struggled with the teaching and challenged Jesus with a question we could all have asked. "How often do I need to forgive my brother, Lord? Seven times?" You can read the whole story in Matthew 18:21–35.

Jesus' reply must have shaken Simon, for what he heard coming from Jesus' lips was, *"Not seven times, Simon, but seventy times seven!"* And that's a Jewish phrase which means *'don't even start counting, there's no limit!'* Jesus knew that if He set a limit of a certain number of times that we would have to forgive, we would simply store up all our venom and hatred and let it all out on, say, the eighth time! The fallen heart of man can't be trusted. Our carnal nature will always try to find a way out of just being obedient.

Also, if there was a limit to the number of times that we have to forgive other people for what they have done to us, then there could also be a limit to the number of times that God would forgive us. And that's something none of us would want to contemplate.

While the people who are forgiven will certainly be blessed by our actions, the primary reason Jesus wanted us to forgive others was so that our own hearts would be set free of the bondage that unforgiveness locks us into. We need to release people from the hook that ties them to us and place them firmly into the Lord's hands for Him to deal with.

There is no doubt that unforgiveness and bitterness is a primary source of stress, pain and, on occasions, physical sickness, and I can tell you from thirty years of experience that it is a primary reason why people who have suffered accidents and traumas are not healed. Even the medical profession recognizes that those who are bitter and unforgiving are more likely to suffer from conditions such as osteoarthritis though, of course, there are also other possible causes for such conditions.

I am sometimes asked whether forgiveness of others means I must then trust the people I've forgiven. The answer is a clear: "No." Once trust has been broken it takes time for it to be restored again. The person who has harmed me needs to prove that it's safe for me to trust them again in the future. I need to know that I will be respected and not taken advantage of.

However, there are some areas of sin, such as sexual abuse, which mean that an offender is not allowed by law to be trusted again with the lives of vulnerable people. This is for their own sake as well as for everybody else's. It is not wise that through misplaced trust they should be released back into a similar area of responsibility and temptation.

Some people don't want to forgive because they see it as excusing the person from any responsibility and accountability for what they have done. But forgiveness is nothing whatsoever to do with escaping justice! If a burglar broke into my house and stole things that were precious to me, I would, of course, be upset and angry. But I would forgive the person who did it, because I wouldn't want to remain in bondage to unforgiveness. Despite me forgiving the person who had done it, if the burglar was caught he should still be brought to justice. He broke the law of the land and should pay the price for what he has done.

Forgiveness releases me from the consequences of bitterness. It doesn't release the burglar from the requirement for justice. I know some people have found it too hard to forgive, especially those who have suffered the kind of terrible things that went on in places like Rwanda. They thought that if they forgave someone, it also meant they had to allow that person to escape all the consequences for what they had done. That is not the case.

The sin of mankind separated the human race from a holy God. We inherited the death sentence (Romans 6:23). The death of Jesus on the cross was an outworking of justice. The price of death was paid – but by a sinless man who couldn't be held beneath the waters of death. Justice was required and justice was carried out. God's desire was for us to be forgiven and restored to a right relationship with Him, but this didn't mean that the requirements of justice could be avoided. God's Son, Jesus, made a way back to God for each one of us who chooses to receive Him as our Savior.

So why did Jesus include a commitment for us to forgive others in a prayer for God to forgive us? He was simply applying what is often referred to as the golden rule – *"Do to others as you would have them do to you"* (Luke 6:31). We all want God to forgive us for the things we have done wrong, the things that are contrary to the law of God. And Jesus is simply saying, if that is how you want God to treat you, then the attitude of your own heart toward those who have sinned against you determines whether or not God is able to answer that prayer.

The greatest blessing that any of us can ever experience, is having our sins forgiven – both in time and eternity. Nothing releases the power of God more immediately or more effectively into our lives than receiving His forgiveness. The cleansing flow of forgiveness from the heart of God truly washes away our sin and makes healing possible in our lives. And when we forgive others the flow of blessing increases! When we forgive others we are releasing them from our sole concern and placing them into the hands of God, to whom we will all have to give an account – and He is the only truly righteous and merciful judge!

Few of us stop to think, when we are being bitter and unforgiving, how deep and dangerous are the consequences of ongoing unforgiveness – especially when tied to bitterness, anger and a desire for revenge. These are Satan's weapons and when we use them against others, they rebound upon us. It has the effect of opening the door of our lives to the work of the enemy. No wonder Paul warned us about not giving a foothold to the enemy (Ephesians 4:27).

When the door of unforgiveness is left open, the consequences can spread much further than our feelings. For it sometimes happens (quite often, in fact) that our body begins to reflect the bitterness in our soul and there are physical consequences. How do I know that? Because of the large number of people I have seen get physically healed when they have chosen to forgive, and they've asked Jesus to set them free from all the consequences of their unforgiveness.

I've met many people who have been abused, injured in accidents caused by other people's carelessness, unjustly accused, betrayed, taken into ungodly relationships or suffered the pain of rejection. Some people were disabled, either physically or psychologically by their experience. Most came for prayer because of their symptoms – everything from depression through to major physical conditions, but there was one pathway on their road to healing that none could avoid treading – the pathway of forgiveness. Perhaps the most difficult individual to forgive is someone who damaged a person they love very much, such as a precious child. But whatever the root of their problem, as they forgave those who had hurt them, the power of God to heal and deliver was released into their life. Each personal story is a miracle of God's amazing grace.

I will never forget teaching on forgiveness at our first major conference in Budapest, Hungary, in June 1991. During that very week, the last of the Russian occupying forces were leaving the country. The people had been crushed by the loss of freedom and direct oppression from the occupying communist forces, and many of them showed signs of that crushing in their bodies, and in the way that they walked. As I looked at the hundreds of people present, my heart went out to them and I longed to see them released from their bondage and able to walk tall again as a free people

There was only one way forward, and I knew I would be walking on sensitive ground when I spoke to the people about choosing to forgive their Russian oppressors. They had all been brought up in the control of the communist system. Many had been treated very cruelly, much of their property had been stolen and even their very identity as creative human beings had been taken from them. They had been robbed. Forgiveness of the Russians was not something they really wanted to think about.

But as I taught from the Word of God, it was clear that the people were understanding the message. If they really wanted to know the release of God's love and power into their lives, they needed to express their forgiveness to their Russian oppressors. Very tentatively, I took them through a prayer of forgiveness, inviting them all to say the prayer with me in their own language. As I did so, I was praying that the Holy Spirit would begin to touch their lives. And He did!

After they had all prayed the prayer, I then prayed with them for healing. I asked that God would release them from the spiritual chains of oppression, and set them free from the control of their spiritual enemy. I had no idea what would happen next. None of us could have anticipated how the power of God would come down on all those wonderful people.

Many were being delivered from the evil one and then I prayed for physical healing as our large ministry team mingled with the people, praying for them one by one and anointing them with oil for healing. It was a totally unforgettable sight. The Shepherd of the sheep was moving amongst His flock, healing, delivering and restoring them. Later in the conference, about 75 per cent of the people present testified that they had been healed of back problems as a result. It was totally extraordinary! God really was setting the captives free. Before our very eyes we were seeing the fruit of what Jesus was teaching about forgiveness. What happened that day was truly miraculous.

We have seen many such days since then – whether teaching a crowd or ministering to the needs of an individual. Jesus knew exactly what He was doing when He included the need to forgive others within the framework of the Lord's Prayer. I know it's hard to forgive those who have been responsible for so much pain in our lives. To forgive others goes against all the natural desires of the flesh. We certainly discover the carnal nature when we choose to follow Jesus – it opposes everything godly in our lives, just like the weeds in our garden oppose the growth of the plants and vegetables we are trying to nurture. The enemy does not want us to forgive, as that releases us from his control. Sometimes we feel able to make a choice to forgive in our mind and with our will, but our emotions take a long time to catch up with our choice. We need to ask Jesus to help us do what is right, for it is the power of God that enables us to forgive.

When there are unforgiveness issues in anyone's life, I usually ask them to write down the names of everyone who was responsible for the suffering they have gone through. This applies just as much to traumas and accidents. Sometimes the list of people to be forgiven can be quite long.

It is necessary to consider those names, one by one, think about what each one has done and then *ask God to help you to* speak out your forgiveness. Finally, with God's help, release each person on your list into the freedom of your forgiveness and ask Jesus to set you free from all the consequences of unforgiveness that there have been in your life. You will be amazed at what God begins to do as a result as He lifts the burden that the enemy has put upon you.

And once you have brought your forgiveness up to date – dealt with everything you know of from the past – then, perhaps, at the end of each day in the future, you could think back over the previous twenty-four hours and speak out your forgiveness to anyone who, on that day, has offended or hurt you in any way.

Forgiving Ourselves

There is one area of forgiveness, however, which all the above does not touch! The fact is that some of the things we struggle with in life had their root in our own choices – the mistakes we ourselves have made. We cannot put the blame for these things on anyone else's shoulders, we need to look at ourselves in the mirror and start forgiving the person who is looking back at us – ourselves!

It is sometimes easier to forgive other people for what they have done, than it is to forgive ourselves for our own mistakes. I've often had to console someone about the consequences of things that they themselves had done, or felt they were responsible for.

Jesus died so that we might be forgiven. He took upon himself the consequences of all the sins and mistakes we have ever made. No sin was excluded from the benefits of the cross. And if we refuse to forgive ourselves, we are telling God that Jesus' death on the cross wasn't sufficient for me and my situation! The sense of personal responsibility for things that have, sadly, gone very wrong can be very great. But unless we start the process of forgiving ourselves and move on, we will be inviting the inner trauma to remain with us for the rest of our lives, becoming a curse on every day we have yet to live.

By not forgiving ourselves we limit the potential for healing that God has for each one of us, we rob ourselves of so much blessing and we rob others of the joy of how different we would be if we could but move on from our past. Every one of us has done things that, subsequently, we have regretted. We need to accept 'self' as an imperfect person and, in humility, add our own names to our forgiveness list!

Time for Action!

Forgiveness does not change history – the facts of what happened will always remain the same, but forgiveness does change how the facts of history affect us now and for every day of the rest of our lives. Going through the doorway of forgiveness is the most powerful healing step anyone can take – especially when it comes to forgiving those who have hurt us on life's journey, through accidents, injuries and emotional traumas that have happened along the way.

So, if you have suffered an accident in the past or have been traumatized through some other situation in life, then may I urge you to spend some time thinking about your situation, what happened to you, whose fault it was – and then do business with God. I can absolutely guarantee that forgiving others is the most important and power-releasing step you could ever take on your journey of healing.

James 1:22–25 advises us, *"Do not merely listen to the word, and so deceive yourselves. Do what it says. Anyone who listens to the word but does not do what it says is like a man who looks at his face in a mirror and, after looking at himself, goes away and immediately forgets what he looks like. But the man who looks intently into the perfect law that gives freedom, and continues to do this, not forgetting what he has heard, but doing it – he will be blessed in what he does."*

One final word – we've often found that some people have a root of bitterness in their heart which is directed at God! They blame Him for allowing the accident to happen and are bitter against Him because of the consequences in their lives. We have found that in these cases it is necessary for people to say sorry to

God for blaming Him for things that are a consequence of us living in a fallen world, which has become such through the choices of mankind at the instigation of the enemy of souls. We cannot blame God for things which are, ultimately, a result of man's sinful choices or Satan's responsibility.

The Key of Deliverance

Setting the Captives Free

When you read the Gospel stories of Jesus, it is so easy to read the accounts of how He healed people through deliverance, and then dismiss the detail of what happened as no longer being relevant to our enlightened day and age! In some strange way people tend to think that the Gospel writers were using the understandings of their day to describe what Jesus was doing because they knew no better. They rationalize away the accounts of Jesus healing people by casting out evil spirits as being influenced by primitive beliefs that have been superseded by modern scientific knowledge!

The biggest problem with this way of thinking is that it assumes that either Jesus didn't know what He was talking about, even though He was the Son of the all-knowing God, with whom He was constantly in touch as He communicated with His Father, or He was deliberately deceiving His disciples, and everyone He was teaching, into believing something that wasn't true!

C.S. Lewis summed up this spiritual dilemma beautifully when he wrote:

A man who was merely a man and said the sort of things Jesus said would not be a great moral teacher. He would either be a lunatic — on

*the level with the man who says he is a poached egg — or else he would
be the Devil of Hell. You must make your choice. Either this man was,
and is, the Son of God, or else a madman or something worse. You
can shut him up for a fool, you can spit at him and kill him as a demon
or you can fall at his feet and call him Lord and God. But let us not
come with any patronising nonsense about his being a great human
teacher. He has not left that open to us. He did not intend to. . . . Now
it seems to me obvious that He was neither a lunatic nor a fiend: and
consequently, however strange or terrifying or unlikely it may seem, I
have to accept the view that He was and is God.* (C.S. Lewis, *Mere
Christianity*, Collins Fontana Books, London 1952, pp. 52–53)

Jesus did know what He was talking about and was not
deliberately deceiving anyone. Jesus described Himself as the
Way, the Truth and the Life. And I have never doubted that when
facing temptation in the wilderness He wasn't just wrestling
with His own inner self, but He was encountering Satan head-
on, who was doing everything he could to make Jesus submit to
him and come under his authority.

Jesus was a total and unprecedented threat to Satan's kingdom,
for as the Son of God on earth, He had never sinned and had
never, therefore, lost His spiritual authority. So He was able to
exercise authority over the servants of Satan, the demons and
evil spirits that all the Gospel writers tell us Jesus cast out of
people. The Genesis prophecy that one day, out of the woman,
would come one who would crush the head of Satan, which
means exercise authority over him, was indeed being fulfilled.
Hence, Satan was desperate to trap Jesus into submission.

But Jesus was aware of every trick of the enemy or "the wiles
of the devil" (KJV) as Paul describes his tricks in Ephesians 6:11,
and resisted him every single time. So, when Jesus encountered
someone in need of healing, and saw that the person was also in
need of deliverance from an evil spirit, He used His authority to
order the spirit to leave, so that the person could then be healed.

Sometimes the person was instantly healed the moment the spirit had gone, while at other times, such as when praying for the woman in Luke 13:10–17 whose spine was bent double, He first ordered the spirit to go and then He laid his hands on her and prayed for her physical healing. In her case deliverance was an essential precursor to her full healing.

In the early days of Ellel Ministries we knew very little about how Satan holds people into bondage through the presence of unclean spirits (also called evil spirits or demons in the Scriptures – they are all the same). But little by little the Lord showed us how Satan can gain access to people's lives in many different ways – sometimes through their own sin, and at other times through the sins of others, including their ancestors – people from previous generations who had opened up the family line to the demonic through things that they had been involved in, such as the occult, Freemasonry, or sexual sin. In the Ten Commandments we read that the sins of the fathers are visited on the children to the third and fourth generations (Exodus 20:5). The way God opened up for the blessings of one generation to be passed on to the next generation is used by the enemy to transfer demonic power down the generational lines in a similar way.

We began to see God bring significant healing through deliverance, and having seen first-hand God transform people's lives in this way, we had no problem in believing that when the Gospel writers described Jesus as casting out evil spirits, then that's exactly what He was doing, casting out evil spirits! It may not sit very well with those who would want to explain away such things with modern-day rational thinking, but when you do what Jesus also taught the disciples to do (in Luke 9:1–2), and discover you get the same results, then the case is already proven. Jesus did set the captives free by delivering them from evil spirits and He's still doing it today! It certainly impacted the Apostle Peter, who preached about it in the Acts of the Apostles: *"You know . . . how God anointed Jesus of Nazareth with the Holy Spirit and power, and how he went around doing good and healing all who were under the power of the devil, because God was with him"* (Acts 10:37–38).

So how is it that people who have suffered accidents or traumas can become the victims of evil spirits? The fact is, at the time these things happen their spiritual defences are often prised wide open by the experience. When we were praying for Lynda, whose story I told earlier in the book, there came a point when she remembered the gap in time between falling off the cliff and landing on the rocks below. While that life-changing journey only took a couple of seconds, that was long enough for the enemy to take advantage of her vulnerability and she felt fear invade her being. There was indeed a good natural reason for being afraid of what was going to happen when she hit the ground, but fear is one of the enemy's prime opportunities for gaining access, and before she hit the ground a spirit of fear had already entered her, from which she would later need deliverance as part of her healing journey.

And, as we have been discovering together, just as a person's body can be broken through the circumstances of an accident, it isn't just the body that suffers the consequences – the spirit and the soul can also be damaged and broken. And wherever there is brokenness there is vulnerability. If there is a split in the hull of a ship, through which water can enter, the water doesn't wait and ask permission before entering! It just takes advantage of the crack in the skin of the vessel and comes in. In just the same way, the enemy is not slow to take advantage of traumas that people experience. For this reason people who have suffered in this way can often need deliverance.

In the account of the woman whose spine was bent double in Luke 13, we are told that she had suffered for eighteen years, which would indicate that something happened eighteen years before which led to the demon getting in and her body being locked into a debilitating infirmity. When I read that story I often think of people I have prayed for whose accidents took place a number of years previously, when a spirit of infirmity had gained access. Jesus prayed for deliverance and saw her set free (*"Woman, you are set free from your infirmity."*). He then laid hands on her for the physical healing of her deformed body, in much the same way as we prayed for Jim and Lynda in the stories told earlier in this book. Without the deliverance it would not have been possible to have prayed effectively for healing.

If that is what Jesus did, then it is right that His disciples should follow His example. That is exactly what we did in those early days of the ministry because we saw in His Word that we have been commissioned by Him to proclaim the Kingdom of God and heal the sick and, where necessary, cast out demons as well (Luke 9:1–2).

For example, there was the couple who had not been able to conceive a child for eleven years, but conceived almost immediately after being delivered of a spirit that had brought death down the lady's generational line. Today the couple have three children, and there are many other previously childless couples around the world who have reason to thank God for the deliverance ministry.

Then there was the lady who was developing chronic arthritis and whose aching joints were a severe limitation on her movement. At the end of the evening she was dancing in thanksgiving for her healing!

And the lady who came to our first major conference, The Battle Belongs to the Lord, with a crippling fear, was wonderfully set free. She then went on to do our nine-week training school before becoming the founding director of the Ellel Ministries center at Pierrepont in southern England, responsible for the NETS training program. When Jesus sets the captives free, He not only heals them but releases them back into their calling and destiny. God's restoration may begin with healing or deliverance, but it doesn't stop there! He has a redemptive plan and longs to see us being fulfilled in it and using all the gifts that He first chose to bless us with.

Whenever I teach about the woman whose spine was bent double, and how she had been bound for eighteen years, I am always reminded of Karen, who stood in front of me at one of our healing services. She had also been bound for eighteen years — since the very beginning of her life. I asked her what her problem was and she told me that the doctors had said there was nothing more they could do for her. She was only eighteen but had an untreatable viral condition affecting both kidneys, for which the only remaining treatment was a double kidney transplant. The medics had advised her that they thought she had less than twelve months to live without such a transplant.

My heart was immediately filled with compassion for Karen as I looked to the Lord for keys on how to pray. Immediately I sensed He wanted me to ask her about her mother, a question that seemed totally unrelated to her condition. I asked the question nevertheless. Karen couldn't tell me anything about her mother, however, because her mother had become pregnant at the age of sixteen and had given the baby up for adoption after the birth.

As she was telling me this, the Lord was speaking to me about her particular situation and I said, "That means you must have been conceived in sexual sin. Have you ever forgiven your natural mom and dad for what they did and have you ever thanked God for your life, and that you weren't aborted?"

Both questions were a surprise to her, but she was more than willing to thank God for her life and then to forgive her parents for their sexual sin. Whereupon I spoke to a spirit of infirmity, just as Jesus had with the woman in Luke 13, and ordered it to leave her. Immediately there was a strong reaction on the inside and then she felt something leave her body.

At this point she had been delivered of the spirit, but her kidneys were still very swollen and painful. Movement, especially bending, was very painful for her. I asked one of the young people's team at Ellel Grange to lay her hands on Karen in the region of the kidneys and pray for healing. She faithfully did this for a full twenty minutes, while I went and prayed with someone else.

At the end of that time we knew that we had witnessed a miracle taking place before our very eyes. The swelling in the kidneys had subsided, the pain had gone, and Karen was able to bend over and touch her toes. She was radiant. Jesus had set the prisoner free. He had healed her body. She wrote to me a few weeks later telling me she had been back to her hospital and the doctors could no longer find any evidence of her condition. So they told her to go and live a normal life and forget what they had said last time!

The stories in the Gospels of what Jesus did when He healed people are examples to us of how He wants us, the Body of Christ, to minister to people in need. Some people live in fear of the enemy, mistakenly thinking that He can come into their lives at any time he likes. But that is not the case. Remember that he can only invade our space if he has been given access, and in broad terms there are only three ways he can do that:

One, as a result of our own sinful choices;

Two, as a result of things that are done to us (such as abuse) or happen to us (such as accidents or traumas) and how we respond in those situations; or,

Three, through a generational inheritance as a result of the sins of our ancestors.

What a privilege it is to be able to share with people the wonderful truths of Scripture, and then see Jesus setting them free to love and serve Him! Deliverance is a vital tool in the equipment box that God has given His Church. It is up to us to use it!

Healing the Broken-hearted

Rebuilding a Shattered Life

So now we can begin to put together all that we have discussed so far to help those who are still living with the consequences of an unhealed past. All of healing is a journey of faith – faith in the God who saves, the God who heals and in the eternal truths that are revealed in His Word.

Foundation Stones

1. SALVATION

The first foundation stone of our journey of faith is coming to Jesus and trusting Him with everything we are. He loved each one of us so much that He unconditionally gave His life that we might live – that we may enter into the salvation that He won for us on the cross. And when we are talking about salvation we are not just talking about being saved, so that when we die we will go to be with Him in Heaven, but also about our journey through life together with Him. And that includes healing, for the very word for salvation can also be translated as healing.

When Isaiah looked forward to the coming of the Messiah, he was able to say that God's salvation would include healing the broken-hearted and setting the captives free (Isaiah 61:1). People who have suffered accidents and been traumatized are often broken-hearted and may also be in need of deliverance.

We begin every one of our Healing Retreats by talking to people about their need of a Savior, that sin may be forgiven and that Jesus should be welcomed as Lord of their lives. This is the entrance gate through which each one of us needs to go in order to receive salvation and enter the Kingdom of God. Jesus expressed this so simply when He was talking to Nicodemus – *"Except a man be born again, he cannot see the kingdom of God"* (John 3:3, KJV). The land of salvation is the inheritance of those who have been born again of God (John 1:12) – and salvation includes healing.

2. FORGIVENESS

The second foundation stone is forgiveness – not only forgiveness for our own sins, but also as detailed in the special prayer Jesus gave to His disciples, forgiving others, in just the same way as we would want Him to forgive us! Bitterness and unforgiveness are an absolute blockage to the flow of God's healing love and power into our lives. Unless we are truly willing to deal with our feelings about anyone who was involved in an accident, or who caused us personal trauma, and have forgiven those involved, our healing will be limited by our own restrictive choices. We will be putting a restriction on what God is able to do for us.

With the two foundation stones of salvation and sincere willingness to forgive in place, we can then turn to pray into the specifics of whatever accident or trauma you have experienced.

Degrees of Traumatic Injury

In broad terms there are three different categories of traumatic injury:

1. *A minor physical injury* which could also have caused some inner trauma to the spirit and the soul as a result of the

physical trauma experienced by the body. This could, perhaps, be the inner equivalent of, say, the physical bruising we may experience when we give ourselves a nasty bang, trip over something and fall on the ground or, perhaps, accidentally hit a thumb with a hammer. This is the sort of trauma that is easily healed with love, care and comfort from those around you. But if injuries such as this occur when a person is very young, and there is no one there to provide the tender loving care which is so essential for children at a time such as this, then the inner being may not heal so easily and may remain traumatized through the additional pain caused by rejection or a lack of love.

2. *A more serious accident or event*, which has caused damage to both the body and the soul resulting in a measure of inner brokenness (broken-heartedness) causing the inner pain to be locked away as a traumatized memory in an injured part of the soul.

3. *A very serious accident or an emotional trauma that was so severe that it has caused complete breaking on the inside.* In these cases the brokenness extends to both the spirit and the soul and the person who is living everyday life today may be completely unaware of the fact that they have part of their personhood (we generally refer to this as a personpart) locked away on the inside. When this happens it is not unusual to find that significant attributes of the personhood, practical talents and giftings, have been locked away on the inside also, leading to a sense of incompleteness, emotional disability or loss of identity. On rare occasions this extent of brokenness can occur as a result of accidents.

Where such brokenness has been caused in children through deliberate abuse it is not unusual for consequential behavioural problems to be evident through the growing years, and for the adult to eventually present to the medical services with psychological or psychiatric symptoms. This is what happened to Sarah, whose story is told in her own book *Sarah: From an abusive childhood to a life of hope and freedom* (**Sovereign World**). This is what we call full fragmentation. It is relatively rare and details of the care and ministry of those who are looking for God's healing from such abusive treatment are outside the scope of this particular book. Sarah's testimony, however, illustrates in a very powerful way how God can bring complete healing from the very worst forms of brokenness.

The majority of traumatic experiences which have left people with long-term unhealed symptoms fall into the second of the above three categories. The suffering can either be from physical symptoms that have not been healed and/or a wide range of behavioural symptoms or feelings such as fear, inner distress, sleeplessness, emotional breakdown, depression and anxiety, or from conditions such as chronic fatigue syndrome, the symptoms of which are well recognized, but for which there is no known physical cause.

It is not unusual for people who struggle with such inner symptoms to feel that life is always a struggle and that they can never truly enjoy being alive. The long-term debilitating effect of unhealed physical symptoms may be a constant reminder of the past and a restriction on living life to the full. The body reflects the inner pain of a broken and unhealed heart. And then the ongoing physical pain causes yet more inner distress in a never-ending debilitating cycle.

Connecting with the Trauma and Breaking the Cycle of Pain

I have written this section as if a person is ministering to themselves, for when people read this book, many will feel as though they need prayer for things they now realize are important and which haven't been properly dealt with in the past. If, however, you are praying with someone else, you need to ensure that each stage of the prayer ministry is carried through effectively.

STEP 1: THE LORDSHIP OF JESUS

Be sure that you fully understand what it means for Jesus to be Lord of your life and you gladly want Him to have this place. You can then pray thoughtfully and meaningfully a prayer such as this:

> *Thank You, Jesus, for dying on the cross for me. I confess that I am a sinner in need of a Savior. I invite You now to be Lord of every area of my life: Lord of my spirit and my relationship with Father God; Lord of my mind and all my thinking; Lord of my emotions and all my reactions; Lord of my will and all my decisions; Lord of my body and all my behaviour; Lord of my sexuality and all my relationships; Lord of my time and Lord of my finances. And Lord of my destiny. I invite You now to rule and reign in my life. I pray this in Jesus's Name. Amen.*

STEP 2: SIN CONFESSED

Be sure that if there is any personal sin associated with the accident which caused your trauma, that it has been fully brought into the light and confessed – not covered up! In Chapter 2 I told the story of the lady who spent sixteen years of unhealed misery having previously never owned up to the fact that she should never have been in the car when her accident happened, for she was on her way to commit adultery. Unconfessed and unforgiven sin gives the enemy access and control. She not only needed healing from the trauma of the accident, but needed deliverance as well.

STEP 3: FORGIVENESS

Ask the Lord to remind you of anyone you need to forgive associated with the events of whatever happened, including any of the medical staff who may inadvertently have caused you additional pain or suffering while trying to help you. And anyone who spoke negative words over you which can act like curses against you. Then don't forget to forgive yourself for everything you did which contributed to the circumstances. People sometimes say things like "I'll never forgive myself" for something they did – which is effectively cursing themselves into never being healed! Jesus died that we may be forgiven – even for the mistakes that we make. If you are struggling with this area, ask the Lord to give you a willingness of heart to face your own personal reality.

STEP 4: CONFRONTING THE BROKENNESS

Ask the Lord to bring the memory of everything that happened at the time of the accident, which has been locked away in the inner brokenness, into the forefront of the mind. At this point you may suddenly feel as though you are right back there at the very moment when the accident or trauma happened. Now is the time to ask the Lord to bind any evil spirits that came in at the time and then take the trauma out of all the memories. You may feel a deep release of emotion taking place as the inner emotions and pain that have lain there unhealed, sometimes for a very long time, are given into the Lord's hands. You may find that you feel tearful or have other feelings linked to the incident. Give yourself time to allow these to be expressed as He heals the broken heart, in accordance with the promise in Isaiah 61:1.

STEP 5: DELIVERANCE

Now take authority over any unclean spirits that may have gained access during the time of trauma, such as spirits of fear, infirmity, or which may have come from people with whom you were closely associated during the trauma. One lady we prayed with was terribly traumatized after watching a horrific car accident taking place and then cradling a dying man in her arms as he passed away at the scene. She was deeply shocked by the experience, and such was her own vulnerability as a result, that when we prayed with her subsequently we had to deliver her of spirits which had come to her from the man who died in her arms. After deliverance always ask the Lord to fill the place that has been vacated by the enemy with His Holy Spirit.

STEP 6: HEALING THE BROKENNESS

Pray for full healing of the inner brokenness – that where some part of your inner being has been shattered by the experience, and traumatized as a result, that the Lord will re-join any broken parts together and put your inner being back into the place of wholeness that it was in, before the accident took place.

STEP 7: PHYSICAL HEALING

Now is the time to pray for physical healing of anything that has remained unhealed since the accident. We would usually take some olive oil, pray over it and ask God to fill the oil with His Spirit. Then anoint the person for healing. When Samuel anointed David with oil to be King, the oil he used had been prepared according to the instructions the Lord has given *"and from that day on the Spirit of the LORD came upon David in power"* (1 Samuel 16:13). We no longer need to prepare oil in the same way as Samuel would have done according to the instructions of the law, for when Jesus went back to Heaven He released the Holy Spirit to the Church at Pentecost, and through the laying on of hands believers can impart God's blessing.

When we were praying for Lynda we went through all the stages described in Steps 1 to 6 above, responding at each stage to what God was doing and then, as I shared in Chapter 6, we anointed her with oil and prayed for physical healing. The Lord had us stand back and watch Him at work as He restored her broken back, supernaturally bending it backwards and forwards until there was no further need, because the spine had been healed. We were watching God perform a miracle in front of a room full of medical professionals, who were having to rethink their medical paradigms as they saw what God did! That was one of those exceptional instances when God was showing us very graphically what He can and does do. In most cases you do not see such a graphic demonstration of God at work! Nevertheless, He is still doing His work on the inside, as is evidenced by the hundreds of testimonies from those whom God has healed, irrespective of whether or not it is as demonstrably visible as it was when He healed Lynda.

Healing for Victims of Wartime Traumas

Post Traumatic Stress Disorder (PTSD)

The history of warfare is littered with accounts of men who returned victorious in battle, but no longer the same person as when they went to war. For example, there are tens of thousands of veterans of the Vietnam War in the USA who have carried the scars of trauma throughout the rest of their lives, many needing intensive psychiatric care and many others still bearing the unhealed scars of battle decades later.

Those who have suffered injury and trauma in wartime situations, as a member of the armed forces, or have suffered injury as an innocent victim of somebody else's battle, form a special category of those who are in need of healing from the traumas they have suffered. Some of those suffering in this way may never have been physically injured, but they are, nevertheless, severely traumatized and can be very broken on the inside as a result of their often horrific experiences.

Many never recover from the emotional and mental distress leading to the need for long-term, even lifelong, medication and treatment. And those who have returned from the battlefront with debilitating physical injuries are not strictly suffering because of an unexpected accident, but because of an injury which has been deliberately inflicted at the hands of an enemy in an attempt to kill them! These are exceptional circumstances, but they are well within the capacity of God to heal and restore.

My first experience of praying for someone who had suffered wartime traumas was an old man who was asking for prayer for healing from a condition he had had for a very long time. I first shared this story in Chapter 3, but I am repeating it here because of its unique relevance to wartime traumas. We had no idea at the time that his condition had its origin in the trenches of the First World War. But God used this man's story to open a door of understanding for me into the terrible inner damage that is caused by the events of war.

As we began to pray I asked the Lord to anoint the ministry with His Holy Spirit. Then I asked the Lord to show the origin of the man's condition. It was soon obvious from his shaking and trembling that something was happening on the inside and God was answering our prayer. Within a few minutes he put his hands out in front of him and began to feel what seemed to be a vertical surface with the flat of his palms. At first it seemed as though he was up against a wall in his imagination, but his face was showing fear and distress. Suddenly the Lord gave us revelation about what was happening. The surface he was feeling for with the flat of his hands wasn't a wall in the traditional sense, but the side of a trench – the trench he had been in when he experienced the events which had traumatized him and affected the rest of his life.

We watched as the part of him which had been broken through the trauma, and locked away for so long on the inside, was feeling in the dark for the top of the trench so he could pull himself up and look at what had happened – most likely the consequences of a shell that had landed very close to where he was. He had been broken by the experience. We had started by asking the Lord to show us where the root of his problem lay. And the Lord had very graphically answered our prayers, showing what it was that we really needed to pray about. His symptoms weren't the real problem – and we needed to pray into the cause of the symptoms.

On another occasion, as first referred to in Chapter 3, I was praying with a man who was part of our team in the early days of the ministry. He had served in the RAF during the Second World War and was part of Bomber Command. He was 'tail-end Charlie' (the rear gunner) on Lancaster Bombers and he was one of the very few such RAF personnel who had served his full quota of thirty-five sorties and had never been shot down. But the price he had paid for this exceptional record as a rear gunner was hidden within his inner brokenness. Many times he had pulled the trigger of his machine gun in self-defence and shot down the pilot of a German fighter aircraft which was intent on destroying his Lancaster. He was a very good rear gunner and the accuracy of his shooting had saved his plane and its crew from certain death on several occasions.

But whenever he had taken the life of a German pilot, as a young Christian man himself, he could not cope with the pain of having just sent another young man into eternity. His only way of coping was to cut himself off from the memory as if it had never happened. But of course it had happened – and the more often we are put in the position of having to bury such pain in further brokenness, the more dysfunctional we eventually become. For the fact is, we cannot ever forget the things that have been part of our lifetime's experiences – they just get buried inside the broken parts which are hiding in the core of our personality.

These memories are part of our life-trace – a continuous spiritual record of everything we have ever said or done. All that we can do is bury the pain and carry on in life as if nothing has happened. However, this results in unhealed inner brokenness. It is not surprising that many ex-military men were never able to talk about the things that they did in the war. Without God's healing, the pain of recovering such memories is more than many men can stand. And they carry on through life functioning as well as they can, but often suffering greatly as a result of the inner damage which has become their unhealed identity.

The consequential distress frequently manifests as frightening nightmares, relived on the video screen of the mind. My friend's subconscious memories fought for recognition and pushed themselves into his nighttime dreams. It is not unusual for such people to regularly wake up screaming, sometimes, even, night after night, as the enemy torments them from within, often making them feel as though they are going mad. It is not surprising that so many people who have been distressed by wartime experiences finish up under medication, and sometimes even in care, for much of the rest of their lives.

When the time came to pray with my friend for healing of the damage caused by his wartime experiences, God took us through an intense learning curve as buried trauma after buried trauma was brought to the light for God to heal. Each painful memory was locked away in a broken part of his soul and when it came to light, the memory was as fresh as it was on the day it had happened. Little by little God brought the memories to the light for healing, until the day came when there were no more unhealed memories and he was able to move on into the rest of his life without fear of any more nightmares. He was completely healed.

At the end of our times of prayer with my friend, all those events that had so distressed him could still be recalled in his mind, but they were now accessible memories which God had healed. God had taken out the trauma from all his experiences and delivered him of the demonic powers that had taken advantage of his distress and held him captive for close on fifty years.

As already mentioned in Chapter 3, I will never forget going with my mother to visit an elderly relative who had been wounded in the First World War. I must have only been about seven years of age, but the memory is still vivid of a man who was only half a man, hallucinating during the daytime, and even though he recognized my mother and she told him who I was, the conversation was a meaningless babble to anyone else. Even as a child I wondered why no one could help him. But there was nothing anyone could do for him, or any of the many other such wartime victims who were living out their lives in an institution, unhealed and unhealable.

Even today, there are countless thousands of ex-military personnel coping in the best way they can with life, receiving the very best medical help that is available from doctors, surgeons, psychologists and psychiatrists, but living in the shadow of devastating unhealed inner brokenness. If Jesus is the Good Shepherd who fulfilled the prophecy of Ezekiel 34:15–16 and the One who would heal the broken-hearted (Isaiah 61:1), and God is the God *of all* comfort, then we should expect those who have been traumatized through war being able to receive the same sort of healing as those who have been traumatized through the more usually experienced accidents of life. The keys to healing are just the same! But the area of forgiveness will need special attention.

No one signs up for the military as a volunteer without being aware of the dangers. The possibility of death and injury are an inevitable consequence of fighting and war. So when it comes to forgiveness, special attention may need to be given to:

i.   Forgiving oneself for deliberately putting oneself into a situation where active duty was a possibility.

ii. Forgiving the more senior officers whose orders led to being in a place of danger.

iii. Forgiving the military and political leaders who took the decision to go to war.

iv. Forgiving the enemy forces and their political masters for taking action that resulted in war.

v. Forgiving the enemy individuals who, in the act of obeying their own orders, brought about the injuries suffered.

vi. Forgiving any enemy individuals who did not adhere to the 'rules of war' and deliberately increased the suffering and consequential injury by inhumane conduct, such as torture, maltreatment of prisoners etc.

vii. Forgiveness for inadequate medical care at the time of greatest need in the battle situation.

viii.Forgiveness where there were insufficient war pensions and long-term poverty as a consequence of injuries received.

ix. And, no doubt, many other issues.

When conscription is in force, men and women are required by law to serve in their country's armed forces, and to cover this an additional forgiveness issue may need to be confronted:

x. Forgiving one's own country for requiring someone to enter military service.

Where injury and suffering have been severe it takes special grace to forgive – but God is able to give that grace if we ask Him. Forgiving does not excuse anyone from their own responsibility before God for what they have done. But it does mean that we are no longer in bondage to either the event or those who caused it. And that is the first step to freedom and consequential healing.

Having dealt with all aspects of forgiveness, then ministering to those who have been traumatized in the military follows exactly the same pattern as for those who have been traumatized through an accident. But the journey to freedom may by necessity have to be a step-by-step process, as little by little all the issues are brought to the Lord for healing.

Epilogue

Restored in the Image and Likeness of God

Long-term pain and suffering can have the effect of changing the focus of our lives. Instead of our identity being in the character, gifts and destiny that God has given us, the limitations caused by our condition become a constant focus of our attention and can have the effect of robbing us of our true destiny.

The deepest level of healing is experienced not just by being healed from something, but by being healed into God's future purposes for your life. Do you remember our foundational definition of healing – *the restoration of God's order in a person's life*? When God's order has been restored we can then begin to look forward to a new destiny with a restored identity – our true identity which is not one focused on a need of healing, but on the blessing of being able to live a life which is now fulfilling God's purposes, and being a blessing to those whom God leads us to love and serve.

Even if there has not been full physical healing following a serious injury, we can still be healed on the inside of all the traumatic consequences, which then enables us to move forward into the purposes of God, irrespective of whether or not we have yet received full physical healing. An inwardly whole person may be able to enter fully into their destiny, even though they may still be praying and waiting for more physical healing!

Beatriz, the leader of the work of Ellel Ministries in Colombia is one such person. She suffered severe spinal damage in an incident when, as a doctor, she was attacked by a patient and thrown down a flight of stairs. Even today she is in a wheelchair and has had many operations to help her cope with her disability. But everyone who knows Beatriz knows also that she is healed on the inside, even if her body has not yet caught up with what God has done. She is a radiant leader who brings hope to many as she trusts God for yet more physical healing. The title of her book is *When the Miracle Comes Slowly* (Sovereign World).

Conversely, there are some people who are physically well, but who are very sick on the inside. They can be gripped by resentment, bitterness and unforgiveness, constantly robbing themselves of God's joy and, as a result, often becoming a burden to all those with whom they are in relationship!

In John 15 Jesus paints a beautiful picture for His disciples of how they have been made clean or, you might say, been healed and restored, through the words that Jesus has spoken to them. They had received truth in their hearts and that truth had transformed their inner beings. Then Jesus urges them to remain in Him so that their lives would become fruitful – for ultimately it is only in and through Him that we will start to display the sort of fruit that will endure. Our lives will then be a blessing in both time and eternity; in time as we and others are blessed as a result of the healing we received, and in eternity, as Father God is blessed by the fruit of His Son's work on the cross. God's healing is always a life-transforming miracle.

One of the greatest blessings we have encountered in the past thirty years of ministry is not only seeing how God heals the broken-hearted, but also how life can begin again for those whom God has healed. What a joy it is to see people's lives being rebuilt, as the Maker intended, when they choose to love and serve the Lord, rediscovering their own true identity and rediscovering the destiny that God has for each one of His children.

Nearly fifty years have passed since I bought the remains of that old Alvis Speed 20. The car still awaits a time when its restoration can be completed – but in the meantime, God has abundantly fulfilled the prophetic vision he gave me as I looked at the wreck of that broken car. Restoring broken lives truly is more important than rebuilding a broken car!

May I encourage you to take to heart personally everything I have shared in this book. You may say, "I have never suffered a major accident" but take some time to think and pray through your own life, asking the Lord to show you any traumatic moments which have left unhealed scars. Then put this teaching into practice and let God begin your own work of personal restoration. You may be very surprised to discover what God does!

A member of our team, for whom praying in this way was a new experience, read an advance copy of this book. And as I was putting the finishing touches to the manuscript I received an email from him in which he says:

> I was praying for a lady who had been born in Bristol in 1942, at the height of the blitz. Due to the bombing, while she was in the womb, she was traumatised and broken inside. This was the first time I have ministered into fragmentation. Your book came to me at just the right time. And your seven-point ministry plan worked extremely well!

My prayer is that you will have many opportunities to be a blessing to others as you use these keys to heal the brokenhearted and set the captives free in Jesus' Name.

ABOUT THE
AUTHOR

Peter Horrobin is the Founder and International Director of Ellel
Ministries. Ellel Ministries International was first established in 1986 as
a ministry of healing in the north-west of England. The work is now (in
2019) established in over thirty-five different countries and students
who have trained with Ellel Ministries are working in every continent
and in well over fifty different countries.

Peter was born in 1943 in Bolton, Lancashire, and was later brought
up in Blackburn, also in the north of England. His parents gave him a firm
Christian foundation for life with a strong evangelical emphasis. His
early grounding in the scriptures was to equip him for future ministry.

After graduating from Oxford University with a degree in Chem-
istry, he spent a number of years in College and University lecturing,
before leaving the academic environment for the world of business
where he founded a series of successful publishing and bookselling
companies.

In his twenties he started to restore a vintage sports car (an Alvis
Speed 20), but discovered that its chassis was bent. As he looked at the
broken vehicle, wondering if it could ever be repaired, he sensed God

asking him a question, *"You could restore this broken car, but I can restore broken lives. Which is more important?"* It was obvious that broken lives were more important than broken cars and so the beginnings of a vision for restoring people was birthed in his heart.

A few years later, he was asked to try and help a person who had been sexually abused. Through this experience God opened up to him the vision for the healing ministry. He prayed daily into this vision until, in 1986, God brought it into being at Ellel Grange, a country house just outside the City of Lancaster. Many Christian leaders affirmed the vision and gave it their support.

Since then a hallmark of Peter's ministry has been his willingness to step out in faith and see God move to fulfil His promises, often in remarkable ways.

Under Peter's leadership, with his wife Fiona, the world-wide teaching and ministry team has seen God move dramatically in many people's lives to bring salvation, hope, healing and deliverance. Together they teach and minister on many different aspects of healing and discipleship.

The work is a faith ministry, depending totally on donations and income from training courses for maintaining and extending the work.

Outside of Ellel Ministries, Peter was the originator and one of the compilers of the amazingly successful and popular **Mission Praise**, now in its 30th Anniversary Edition. It was originally compiled for Billy Graham's *Mission England* in 1984.

He is also an enthusiast for fishing and classic cars. His **Complete Catalogue of British Cars**, which was first published in 1975, has long been a standard reference work on the history and technical specification of every model of every make of British car manufactured between 1895 and 1975! During his years in academic life he also wrote and edited books of specialist technical interest about different aspects of building science and technology.

Peter wrote the teaching contained within the online training programme *Ellel 365*. This is being relaunched, both online and in book form, as *Journey to Freedom*. This 260-part programme provides daily input to those seeking healing, training and an understanding of what it means to be a follower and disciple of Jesus. Many have testified to the life-transforming blessing it has brought to their lives.

The full story of Peter's life and ministry is now told in his latest book, *Strands of Destiny*.

For details about the current worldwide activities of
Ellel Ministries International please go to:
ellel.org

Further books by Peter Horrobin

Healing Through Deliverance
The Foundation and Practice of Deliverance Ministry

In this ground-breaking book, Peter Horrobin draw on his thirty years of experience of ministry to lay out the biblical basis for healing through deliverance.

He provides safe guidelines for ministry, helps the reader identify demonic entry points and teaches how we can be delivered and healed from the effects of demonic power. His prayer for the reader is that their commitment to Christ will be deepened and that they will respond afresh to God's call to heal the broken-hearted and set the captives free.

Hardback 630 pages, £24.99, ISBN 978-1-852404-98-7

Forgiveness – God's Master Key

Forgiveness is key to the restoration of our relationship with God and to healing from the consequences of hurtful, damaging human relationships. From the cross, Jesus prayed these dramatic words to God, "Father, forgive them, for they do not know what they are doing." Learning to forgive others is the beginning of a lifetime's adventure with God – it really is the most powerful prayer on earth!

Paperback 110 pages, £6.99, ISBN 978-1-852405-02-1

Healing from the consequences of Accident, Shock and Trauma

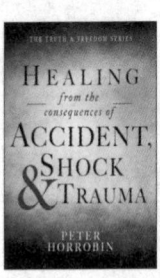

Traumatic events leave a scar on broken lives. Unhealed trauma is one of the primary reasons why some people do not easily heal from the consequences of accidents or sudden shocks. This ground-breaking book is the culmination of thirty years of experience praying for such people. Peter carefully explains what trauma can do to people and how to pray for healing. This foundational teaching has been instrumental in bringing permanent healing to people all over the world. An essential manual for those who regularly pray for people – a life-transforming handbook for those who are struggling themselves with unresolved and unhealed issues – including the consequences of shock and injuries sustained in the military.

Paperback 176 pages, £9.99, ISBN 9781852407438

Living Life God's Way

'Living Life God's Way' is an immensely readable and practical book. In this revised and updated edition of 'Living the Life – Practical Christianity for the Real World', Peter Horrobin draws on his thirty-five years of Christian leadership to present the reader with a practical guidebook for living the Christian life. Peter uses real life testimonies, parables and illustrations to unlock some of the most difficult of life's issues, that often make us stumble through our Christian walk. What never seemed to make sense is suddenly crystal clear – even for the most experienced Christian, helping all of us to discover how to Live Life God's Way!

This book was written to help new Christians get established in their faith and to provide older Christians with the kind of realistic help that is needed to keep their lives on track with God.

Paperback 222 pages, £10.99, ISBN 978-1-85240-758-2

Strands of Destiny
How God used a crashed car to envision and build a ministry that touches the nations

Strands of Destiny is Peter Horrobin's personal story of how God prepared him for his life's calling, envisioned him through the remains of a crashed car and finally established the work of Ellel Ministries at Ellel Grange in 1986. This extraordinary and often miraculous story, will build your faith as you journey with Peter through the ups and downs of an amazing spiritual adventure.

Every chapter is a testimony of thanksgiving for the amazing love and provision of God.

Paperback, 440 pages including 48 pages of photographs, ISBN: 9781852408350

Other books by Peter Horrobin available from SovereignWorld.com

The Truth Stick

A Parable for Adults and Children

This is a truly enchanting story of Ratty, Mole and Badger and the adventures they have discovering the amazing secrets that lie hidden in Wild Winters Wood! Ratty's question "What is truth?" reveals the answers every child needs to know. Whether young or old, you will be delighted with this refreshing tale.

Hardback 128 pages, £9.99, ISBN 0-9546380-1-8

The Parables of Harris

Lessons from the Real-life Adventures of a Black Labrador by Peter and Fiona Horrobin

From the founders of Ellel Ministries International comes this amusing and entertaining book about Harris, their black Labrador. "From the day Harris came home our lives were changed for ever! From the moment he put his first huge paw over our threshold, and took control of the home, we knew we were in for an adventure!" And his adventurous exploits have become modern-day parables of life.

Paperback 128 pages, £6.99, ISBN 0-9546380-0-X

Most books are also available in e-book format and can be purchased online.

BOOK 4 JESUS OUR LIVING HOPE ISBN 978 1 85240 7612

The heart of Book 4 is, simply, Jesus. We look at the prophe-
cies about the coming Messiah, Jesus's early life, His temptations, the beginnings of His ministry and the call and commis-
sioning of His disciples. Then we learn deep lessons from the
final teachings Jesus shared with His disciples. A hugely
practical book in the series, full of life-application teaching.

BOOK 5 JESUS HEALER AND DELIVERER ISBN 978 1 85240 7964

Book 5 focuses on all the different healings that Jesus carried
out and on the different healing principles we can learn from
the things that Jesus said and did when healing and delivering
people. We see how Jesus seamlessly blended inner healing,
physical healing and deliverance ministry as He sought to
bring wholeness into the lives of those who came to Him.

BOOK 6 DYING TO LIVE ISBN 978 1852407704

All the Gospels culminate in the amazing accounts of Jesus's
death and resurrection. We look stage by stage at all that Jesus
did for us on the cross and examine just what His sacrifice
means for us today. The Great Commission, the life of the
early church, all that Jesus taught about the end times and His
coming again complete this book in the series.

BOOK 7 GOD'S PLAN FOR MY LIFE ISBN 978 1852407858

In Book 7 we see how all the teaching of Books 1-6 together
help us focus on how God wants heal each one of us on our
Journey to Freedom. In a very practical way we look at the
main areas of life where people most need healing and see
how, through healing, God enables us to both face the reality
about our past and equip us for the future He has planned for
our lives.

BOOK 8 MY LIFE IN GOD'S HANDS ISBN 978 1852408503

The last book in the series concentrates on how to live in
God's vision for our lives and how to persevere in running the
marathon race that life is for each one of us. We then look at
the final stages of life and the challenge of finishing our race
well as we prepare for our eternal destiny and the glorious
future that lies ahead for those who are in Christ Jesus.

For details of many more books published by Sovereign World Ltd, please visit our online shop to browse our range of titles.

www.sovereignworld.com

Or write to the company at the headquarters address:

Sovereign World Ltd, Ellel Grange, Bay Horse, Lancaster, LA2 0HN, UK

info@sovereignworld.com

About Ellel Ministries International

Ellel Ministries
International

Our Vision

Ellel Ministries is a non-denominational Christian Mission Organization with a vision to resource and equip the Church by welcoming people, teaching them about the Kingdom of God and healing those in need (Luke 9:11).

Our Mission

Our mission is to fulfil the above vision throughout the world, as God opens the doors, in accordance with the Great Commission of Jesus and the calling of the Church to proclaim the Kingdom of God by preaching the good news, healing the broken-hearted and setting the captives free. We are, therefore, committed to evangelism, healing, deliverance, discipleship and training. The particular scriptures on which our mission is founded are Isaiah 61:1–7; Matthew 28:18–20; Luke 9:1–2; 9:11; Ephesians 4:12; 2 Timothy 2:2.

Our Basis of Faith

God is a Trinity. God the Father loves all people. God the Son, Jesus Christ, is Saviour and Healer, Lord and King. God the Holy Spirit indwells Christians and imparts the dynamic power by which they are enabled to continue Christ's ministry. The Bible is the divinely inspired authority in matters of faith, doctrine and conduct, and is the basis for teaching.

**For full details about the world-wide work of
Ellel Ministries International, please visit our website at:**

www.ellel.org

or write to:
Ellel Ministries International
Ellel Grange
Ellel
Lancaster, LA2 0HN
United Kingdom

Would You Join With Us To Bless the Nations?

At the Sovereign World Trust, our mandate and passion is to send books, like the one you've just read, to faithful leaders who can equip others (2 Tim 2:2).

The 'Good News' is that in all of the poorest nations we reach, the Kingdom of God is growing in an accelerated way but, to further this Great Commission work, the Pastors and Leaders in these countries need good teaching resources in order to provide sound Biblical doctrine to their flock, their future generations and especially new converts.

If you could donate a copy of this or other titles from Sovereign World Ltd, you will be helping to supply much-needed resources to Pastors and Leaders in many countries.

Contact us for more information on (+44)(0)1732 851150 or visit our website www.sovereignworldtrust.org.uk

"I have all it takes to further my studies. Sovereign is making it all possible for me"

Rev. Akfred Keya – Kenya

"My ministry is rising up gradually since I have been teaching people from these books"

Pastor John Obaseki – Nigeria